We have never had su  ra-
tion. Just look at m   ; a
different kind of boo   .ies
of the authors as well ....g uns book caused me to
feel like I wanted to start out all over again, maybe even get saved
again. Why? This book is about adventure, great risk, total yielding-
ness, obedience; really, it's about abandoned lives to God. And the
results are amazing: salvations, healings, changed lives, changed
communities. Wow! I longed to go with them, but the trips were
already completed. It's about legacy, amazing legacy, biblical-like
stories of legacy to pass on to others. It's compelling, convicting,
amazing, and miraculous. I could hardly put the book down. Pick
this book up to read and it will stick to your hand like glue until
you finish it.

—**Barbara J. Yoder**
Lead Apostle
Shekinah Regional Apostolic Center
Breakthrough Apostolic Ministries Network
www.shekinahchurch.org
www.barbaraYODERblog.com

Are you longing to walk closer with God? Let Lana Heightley and
Melonie Janet Mangum be your personal guides as they share stories
of their thrilling journey with God. In this insightful book, they
will show you what your life can be like with Jesus. You will be
challenged as they take you along on their adventures with the Holy
Spirit. You will be edified as they share the deep, rich, and exciting
lessons they have learned along the way. And, you will be inspired
as you read the captivating testimonies of God's power, love, and
faithfulness. Buy this book today. You will be glad you did!

—**Dr. Rev. Diane Wigstone**
Author
Founder, Destiny Center
President, YWAM Hollywood

Special operators Melonie Janet Mangum and Lana Heightley have written a must-read for those called to disciple the nations for Jesus Christ. Special operators are the military's elite of the elite who are able to complete missions deep in enemy-controlled territory. Janet and Lana are cut of the same cloth. They have a passion for saving souls by bringing men and women into the kingdom of our Lord and Savior Jesus Christ. Their apostolic special operations for Christ have taken them to some of the most dangerous regions on earth. Living lives of faith, divine appointments, and nerve-wracking danger, these two are leaving a treasure trove of experiential wisdom to the generations that are willing to walk in their footsteps.

—Dr. Rev. Bill Peters
Cofounder, Angel Fire Christian Center
and the International Children's Aid Network

Read this book with expectation. Janet and Lana share powerful experiences filled with humor and leadership lessons learned from their first hand encounters with the mission field. These experiences and powerful truths will enrich the life of every reader. The amazing journey of Janet and Lana will challenge you to dare and believe, yes, you can do more than you ever dreamed. The passion and anointing from these pages will definitely transform your legacy.

—Rev. Dr. Naomi Dowdy
Founder Chancellor, TCA College, Singapore
Former Senior Pastor, Trinity Christian Centre, Singapore
Speaker, Author, Mentor, Trainer, Consultant

I'm extremely blessed to have ministered overseas with both Lana and Janet, and I can attest they are amazing Women of God! I have witnessed firsthand the power of their ministries, and the anointing they both carry as warriors in God's kingdom. These stories will fill you with hope and a new understanding of God's grace at work around the world. As they have fired up my life and ministry as mentors, I'm confident you will be fired up as well, once you read this book and see God's amazing power in action.

—**Rev. Merrily Dente Madero, BSME, BA, MS**
Ordained Minster, Assembly of God
Retired Colonel, USAF
President, M3 International

I have spent the last twenty years of my life encouraging women to step into their ministry callings. It has not been an easy assignment for me, since so much of the church still believes women should be limited in their influence and outreach. Thankfully when I get discouraged, I end up meeting another dynamic woman who is living out what I have been preaching. Janet Mangum and Lana Heightley are two women who have inspired me since the very beginning of my journey. I will never forget when I taught them in a class on Women in Ministry in Colorado. I knew they were full of the Holy Spirit's fire, and that they were going to blaze a trail for Jesus! This book is the story of that trail-blazing adventure. You will love reading about all the ways God used them in their missionary endeavors. My prayer is that this book will inspire many people—especially more women—to leave fear behind and to do the works that Jesus did. He uses surrendered vessels, regardless of gender, race, or class. As you read, let God strip away the restrictions you have placed on yourself. Then pray, "Here I am, Lord, send me."

—**J. Lee Grady**
Author and Director of The Mordecai Project
LaGrange, Georgia
Contributing Editor, Charisma Magazine

The Word became flesh and dwelt among us. He, Jesus, then promised the Comforter to lead and guide us as we become his ambassadors to the nations. Through the apostle Paul to William Carey and now through these women, Jesus continues to call the nations to his side. I have watched thousands of missionaries and ministers come and go and realize faithfulness is a rare commodity among those who trek through the continents to take the gospel to the least reached. Lana's and Janet's stories and encounters are real, unsanitized, and glorious. My hope is that their legacy will inspire you to run as they have—until every home has heard the gospel.

—Riaan Heyns
Vice President of Major Partnerships
Every Home for Christ

UPSHIFT

The Holy Spirit's Unfathomable Power Revealed

REV. DR. LANA C. HEIGHTLEY
REV. DR. MELONIE JANET MANGUM

Foreword by Rev. Powell H. Lemons

bookV**ill**ages

ISBN: 978-1-94429-869-2

Cover and Interior Design by Scot McDonald
Cover image: iStock.com/brightstars
Lana Heightley bio photo: Kristen Michalski

LCCN: 2020917166

Printed in the United States of America

1 2 3 4 5 6 7 8 9 10 2020 24 23 22 21 20

Even though these are our stories,
they are not about us—
they are testimonies to God's glory.

In memory of my father, who took his first mission trip
when he was sixty-nine years old. He contributed
greatly to my love for missions.
Lester Lemons (1910-1997)

And for my brother, who taught me how.
Powell H. Lemons (1945-)

Lana Heightley

I dedicate this book in honor of all those who have believed
in me. Their names may not be in each story, but their
encouragement and support were integral to the support
system that afforded me the amazing invitations of the Holy
Spirit.

Melonie Janet Mangum

CONTENTS

FOREWORD

While I have written many forewords in my career, none gives me greater joy than this one.

Hold on to your holy seat! You may not believe what you will read in this book, but it is the ironclad truth. The stories recounted have been verified by a number of people, including me. Read each chapter with an open heart and praise to God.

I have known Lana Heightley all her life—I am her brother. She has developed a powerful ministry of missions teams overseas, holding empowering conferences and training thousands of women throughout the world to know they are called for a purpose, and know God has a plan for their life. Thousands upon thousands have been blessed and trained in Africa, Japan, India, the Philippines, and beyond—forty nations in all. Called as a teen, she did not come to the fulfillment of that calling until years later. But God had his plan.

When I first met Janet Mangum, she was on staff as an associate pastor of a substantial church that had developed a worldwide missions department. She truly (genuinely) had a heart for God. Then she took her first outdoor evangelistic crusade in the Philippines in 1999 and has not looked back. After trips to thirty-five countries—some, more than twenty-five times—she became director of transformation for Aglow International. Through this ministry, over 83,000 lives have been changed dramatically, and in partnership with local ministries, many churches have been planted.

I am delighted to recommend Lana and Janet to you, and this book for your edification and amazement. While it may read like a continuation of the book of Acts, it is a reminder that our Lord once said that we would do his works, too.

Read on, my friend, and be blessed. Of course, all glory to God.

—Rev. Powell H. Lemons, BA, MDiv
Retired Pastor

THANK YOU

Karen Roberts, my (Lana) amazing soul editor friend who makes me look good. She is my midwife for stories delivered. I would never consider writing a book without her amazing talent and wisdom. You are the best!

Karen Pickering, publisher, whose loving guidance was most excellent. When we needed encouragement, enlightenment, and engagement, she was the go-to person. Easy, energetic, and always ready to give valuable feedback. Thank you.

Lora Schrock, what a professional! Your splendid editing was first class. Thanks for your patience.

Diane Wigstone, who was the impetus for writing our stories. You were our accountability. Your monthly mentoring meetings were filled with instruction and were priceless. Thanks for your sincere heart gift. Hugs to you, our dear friend.

A heartfelt thanks to the following team members (and amazing friends) who witnessed some of the story content and who also gave encouragement to me (Lana) and much needed prayerful support. We have walked through the nations together. Thank you to Sue Chamberlain, Sherry Elliott, Brenda (Pat) Johnson, JoAnne Meckstroth, Wendi Moen, Debbie Scroggin.

THOUGHTS FROM THE AUTHORS

This book is fruit of the seeds God planted and watered many years ago when he chose us, two humble homemakers, to become living expressions of his love and power. Though we were young wives and mothers, God gifted us for purposes we could not imagine. In his time, he sent us out to the nations. Some things cannot be learned by instruction alone. They require adventure to fulfill the understanding. We can attest to this life-giving principle.

Personal Thoughts from Lana

It has been a great undertaking for Janet and me to reflect on our lifelong personal journey with God. We feel compelled, in this unique time in history, to share our experiences as they relate to the mission field worldwide and the dramatic upshifts the Holy Spirit has so graciously infused into our experiences. Our intent is to encourage each of you to recognize that God is bigger than the circumstances you face. He has a plan and destiny for you, as well. Also, we want to leave a record of our legacy for our families and the generations that follow (us). We acknowledge that some of our stories are beyond belief. Strange but true, one might say. We have written them as well as possible. We were there.

Our stories will introduce you to many gifted, fascinating women who are making a difference for God's kingdom in their spheres of influence. All followers of Christ are gifted differently, unique in their strengths and weaknesses. God warns us not to covet the gifts of others. Instead, we are to join with them, using our uniqueness in him. Teamwork with both the Spirit of God and others is key. Together, we are strong.

Janet and I are thankful that God brought us together thirty years ago. We live eighteen hundred miles apart, yet we are in touch continuously, as one family. Blessed to minister in over forty countries and speak to thousands of people, we see how God has been faithful and consistent to supply provision, protection, and his presence. We have depended on him and believed he would give us both his messages to be shared and a spirit for impartation.

Our stories demonstrate how the Good News, combined with discipleship, breaks down evil strongholds and releases the once confused, bound, and tormented to lead in the advance of his kingdom. One of our goals in writing this book includes encouraging you in the providence of God as you are led by his Spirit. His providence has been astounding. Sharing these few stories, only a portion of our many incredible experiences, has reminded us of the many ways in which he makes a way where there seems to be none.

We have tasted the overriding, extravagant purpose and generosity of our heavenly Father for his family. Our Lord Jesus has kept his promise to never leave or forsake us. The indwelling Holy Spirt has led us in surprising, often shocking, and innovative ways. May these stories encourage you that when you feel you can't hear his direction clearly, understand his goals fully, or comprehend his ways completely, he is working behind the scenes. You are family. He is with you. You will hear his voice. You will find yourself following his lead, even when you aren't sure it is his leading. And like Janet and me, you will rejoice and marvel at his goodness through your years.

"Blessed are you among women," declares the angel Gabriel to Mary (Luke 1:42). His blessing was followed with a command to rejoice. Before he told her why he was there, he urged Mary to give thanks. He knew he was bringing good news, the best news. Mary trusted and rejoiced before she understood. She had no idea this shocking, glorious, and life-changing news would impact the entire world. Rather than worrying, Mary chose to trust the Lord and gave thanks with heartfelt sincerity: "My soul magnifies the Lord, and my spirit has rejoiced in God my Savior . . . For He who is mighty has done great things for me, and holy is His name" (Luke 1:46-47, 49, NKJV).

Mary's beautiful prayer of gratitude is an example of giving thanks, not because she had it all figured out, because she certainly did not. She trusted the Father and his providential goodness.

Trusting the Holy Spirit's lead is the key to our moving forward in his plan, his purpose, and his powerful demonstration of life.

We trust these stories will stir your hearts and minds into rejoicing. Our hope is that though you cannot see the final outcome, you will actively pursue what you cannot imagine at the moment. May the Holy Spirit develop a burning desire within you to be all that God has called you to be and do. The younger generation is watching to see how we walk with our Creator, Redeemer, Deliverer, and the Spirit Who indwells and imparts eternal, transforming life.

Personal Thoughts from Janet

Powell, Lana's brother, describes his sister's thinking, writing style, and strategy as flowing streams. And he describes mine as thinking in chunks of contrast. As different as Lana and I are, working together has continually brought life, blessing, and victory. You will see how diverse our writing voices are throughout the stories in this book, yet you will also see our single purpose in relating the grace and power of Jesus.

As romantic as some of the locations of these stories' settings may seem, we have endeavored to create accurate depictions of our experiences—not only the victories, but also the doubts, pains, and struggles in the process. We have been gut-honest (totally honest). The realities of each situation gave God a glorious opportunity to display his miraculous power, love, and care for his family. Lana always told us that following the Holy Spirit meant everything could drastically change every ten to fifteen minutes. Our stories show the reality of the need for continual flexibility in hearing and responding to the Holy Spirit.

The personal stories we read in the Bible may be described as sad, harsh realities. Often, we want to skip those paragraphs or chapters and move forward into something more positive and affirming. However, the stories of those who have passed through the fires of pain and sorrow portray authentic situations and are there for a purpose. As we read about their journeys, we feel the power of the wind of the Spirit drawing us upward into the embrace of our heavenly Father. We have endeavored to do the same with our stories.

Sometimes we would experience a downhill descent of confused unbelief knocking at our door. However, as we persevered and continued to trust in the Lord, we began to sense the upshift and victorious joy his presence brings, much like flowers blooming alongside a dusty roadway. As we look back, remembering individuals, landscapes, and personal intentions, we worship our profound and indomitable God. With great fervor, we exclaim the chorus, "Through it all, we've learned to trust in Jesus. We've learned to trust in God."

We have experienced the constant love and power of the Father, through the sacrifice of his Son, portrayed by the Holy Spirit, in the details of each story. The gap invitations morphed into his glory stories. We pray and hope our stories defeat the enemy's lies of disqualification, strengthen your resolve in the middle of uncertainty, and validate the deliberate and relational love of your heavenly Father in all your upcoming journeys.

Heritage and Timing

Because He Said . . .

"All the days ordained for me were written in your book before one of them came to be." (Ps. 139:16)

"'For I know the plans I have for you,' declares the Lord, 'plans to prosper you and not to harm you, plans to give you hope and a future.'" (Jer. 29:11)

"For we are God's handiwork, created in Christ Jesus to do good works, which God prepared in advance for us to do." (Eph. 2:10)

"There is a time for everything . . . a time to be born and a time to die." (Eccles. 3:1-2)

* * *

One thing I am certain of is God has an amazing plan and destiny for each of us. Over the years, I have come to understand my heritage and my place in God's great family. It has been and continues to be an unfolding revelation.

When I was fourteen years old, God gave me a vision of how I would serve him. This vision came in the summer of 1957 at a youth camp in the beautiful San Bernardino Mountains of Southern California. I thought by the time I had finished high school, I would go directly to the mission field. It didn't quite happen that way. My heritage would be revealed to me over a period of many years. From the first vision of involvement in missions until I took my first trip was twenty-eight years.

God's Timing

Everything God does is on his time schedule. Ecclesiastes 3:1 says, "There is a time for everything, and a season for every activity under the heavens." The coming of the promised Messiah was in God's appointed time. "But when the set time had fully come, God sent his Son, born of a woman" (Gal. 4:4). The Lord Jesus himself had to surrender his circumstances to his Father's timing. At the wedding in Cana, Jesus said to his mother, "My time has not yet come" (John 2:4, GNT). When his brothers urged him to go to Judea and make himself known, he replied, "The right time for me has not yet come" (John 7:6 GNT).

God's timing is always perfect. The Bible proves it over and over. But in our humanness, we have difficulty waiting for the right time in our (own) circumstance. At some point all of us have lacked knowledge in dealing with the issue of timing. Maybe it is more the issue of *waiting* on God's timing.

Sarai, Abram's wife, was no exception. God appeared to her husband and told him to count the number of stars in the heavens (Gen. 15) so he could see how numerous his offspring would be. Sarai was so excited by such a great promise, she thought she was ready to help carry out the promise. But many years passed without (hearing) the sound of a baby's cry. After the revelation of the promise, the delay Sarai suffered brought great disappointment. God had said there would be a son, yet there had not been one.

Not understanding God's timing, Sarai decided to take matters into her own hands. She arranged for Abram to sleep with her maidservant Hagar (Gen. 16). The maidservant conceived and bore him a son. Can you imagine how Sarai felt when Hagar's son

Ishmael was born? As she longingly looked upon the new mother and son, she must have wondered, *Why not me, Lord? You promised I would have a son.*

Thirteen years later, when Abram was ninety-nine years old (Gen. 17), God appeared to him and reconfirmed his covenant with him. At this time, he changed Abram's name to Abraham, and Sarai's name to Sarah. He added his name into theirs, creating their covenant names. So, "at the appointed time" (Gen. 18:14), Sarah did have a son, Isaac, through whom God's promise was fulfilled.

I did not understand the principle of timing in the revelation of my heritage in God's family either. Like Sarah, I expected it to happen in my time frame.

My Calling

I was born into a family with a wonderful Christian mother, the greatest blessing a person could receive. From my earliest childhood memories, I visualize my mother sitting on the living room couch reading her Bible and praying every morning. She was my first mentor and teacher. She taught me about the things of the Lord as I grew during my young, tender, impressionable years.

In my youth I was like many of the committed Christian young people around me who were idealistic about life. I believed God had great plans for me, though no one in my immediate family had graduated from high school. All I needed was his showing me the plans, and I would be on my way. His lessons on timing were only beginning to unfold.

My missions journey began at youth camp. I heard a heart-stirring message about giving everything to Christ. As I was praying at the altar, it was as though I had fallen suddenly into a trance. I saw a huge globe with the nations of the world. Then I saw Jesus standing to the left in white clothing, with his right hand outstretched to the globe. His eyes were intently upon me. I knew he was asking me to go to the nations as his representative. I was his daughter, and he had chosen me. My heritage in him was to be revealed to the world soon—or so I thought.

To my surprise, a picture of a small village where older women and small children sat on wooden benches came next in my vision. I saw myself standing in front of the people, teaching them with my Bible in my hand. Thatched huts and palm trees encircled them. I didn't recognize the people group, as I had not traveled anywhere outside my small sphere. But they appeared to be of Asian culture, brown-skinned, and weathered by the sun.

The vision was vivid, and I knew it was from God. I cried out to him like the Old Testament prophet Isaiah, "Here am I, Lord, send me!" (Isa. 6:8).

I thought my ministry would blossom immediately after high school, but I didn't understand the principle of God's timing. Similar to young David before he became king, I needed training and proving time. I knew nothing about faithfulness, character building, how to take the first step, divine appointments and alignments, how to embrace life's experiences, the commands of God, or any of the other principles addressed in this book. Like Sarah, I saw no immediate fruit from the vision I had. I experienced endless days of disappointment and nagging heart pain. I spent the next several years feeling as though I had failed God, and I allowed guilt to plunder my days.

I chose to marry and have children. As the years passed, I often stayed home when my pastor announced that a visiting missionary was speaking in our church services. I could not bear the grief of the unfulfilled promise. I loved the Lord passionately. I studied his Word. Yet I lived with the lack of fruit from my vision.

To overcome my emptiness, I decided to help in Sunday school classes. I began in the church nursery. I was faithful with what my hands found to do. Before long, I advanced to teaching older ages. Eventually I taught in all the departments and reached the college and career classes.

In the meantime, my hunger for the knowledge of his Word led me to attend evening Bible college classes. It was a heavy load, working a full-time job, and raising my two sons. In the middle of the busyness, I didn't realize God was training me for his plan. He was giving me opportunities to develop the leadership qualities he had given me.

As a young child, I had been a good student, usually making As. I was athletic and liked by my classmates. I held leadership positions in my school. For twenty-five years, finances required me to work outside the home as an administrative assistant. All those experiences gave me interpersonal, leadership, and administrative skills—absolute requirements for what I would do one day, taking teams around the world to teach biblical principles to national leaders.

My husband, John, was employed in the high-tech computer industry, and due to the nature of his business, we moved several times through the years. The moving caused me to leave behind many treasured friendships. I am a very relational person, so each move increased the sadness in my heart. I often wondered, *Why can't I stay in one place so I can develop long-term friends and have stability in my life?* I even complained to the Lord about the moves.

Little did I know God was developing relationships with individuals who would become my ministry partners years later. After I began taking teams to the nations, I realized the advantage the moves had been for me. I had met powerful women of God in each place.

God knows how to prepare us for the work he has assigned to us as his daughters and sons. His timing is perfect.

My First Missionary Journey

Almost thirty years after my visitation from the Lord during summer camp, I made my first missionary journey as a direct result of my earthly family heritage. When I was a young girl, I had no idea how my heritage would unfold. This trip to the Philippines was at the request of my younger brother Powell, who had become a pastor, annually partnering with my lay-missionary father. There I ministered to the same people group I had seen in the vision. God's timing of his promise had come.

I still get emotional when I think about it. For my first assignment on the field, I was sent to a small village in the northern part of Luzon, the main island in the Philippines. As I approached the village, I came to a little nipa hut. A small group of people waited on benches for me. I was so overwhelmed, I could do nothing but cry. To my surprise it was the same vision of my youth—the same little village, benches, and dark-skinned people. How the goodness of our God rushed through my soul.

At that moment, I realized that while my timing was not his timing, his faithfulness to do what he promised came in the fullness of his time. That first missionary trip was in 1986, beginning the fulfillment of my vision, and I have served the nations since (then).

For the next nine years, I ministered in the Philippines, sleeping on mats and traveling across the island country. I preached and taught at universities, small villages, schools, governmental offices, factories, and churches. During that time, I saw thousands of people come to the crusades. I prayed with many to receive Christ into their hearts, and many received physical healing.

Women With A Mission

One morning in 1994, as I was home making my bed, I was watching a newscast featuring a report on a women's conference in Beijing, China. It was reported that approximately 30,000 women attended. The speakers promoted beliefs that conflicted with biblical principles. My heart was grieved. I fell across an ottoman and cried out to God, *Where is* your *great army of women?*

I thought about the crusades where I had taught in the Philippines. There was advanced biblical training and seminars for men, but nothing similar for women. God was birthing in me a desire to see women trained to win their nations for Christ. I asked God, *How can I offer these women leadership training so they can reach their own people?* As I prayed, I saw that God was preparing a great army of women to carry the gospel message to their own nations. At that moment, I realized God was calling me to organize women to teach and train women.

Women With A Mission (WWAM), a nonprofit missions organization based in Colorado Springs, Colorado, was founded in 1996, the year I took my first team of American women overseas. The ministry was formed to send women who have been specifically called by God to train and equip women of Third World countries to become leaders for Christ in their nations. To date, God has placed about sixty leaders in my life whom I mentor intentionally, in the US, and around the world.

Currently, WWAM sends teams of women to minister—moms, singles, and pastors. The women, ranging in age from nineteen to eighty, conduct seminars, workshops, conferences, and crusades for Third World women in their villages, towns, and countries. In the past several years, the ministry has expanded to include conducting pastors' conferences. And the Lord has also opened doors in many other nations, including Australia, Italy, Israel, Japan, and Malaysia.

I am especially thankful for the opportunity to disciple women everywhere in the knowledge of Christ. The Lord has given me the opportunity to raise up and equip women to reach their nations for the sake of the gospel. And through WWAM, I have the privilege of taking American women on their first missionary journey, also. It is extremely rewarding to train them in the work of missions, especially in cross-cultural experiences.

The Increase

The WWAM ministry has expanded greatly since the early years. Now, it is not unusual to have teams crisscrossing Europe,

Asia, and Africa to conduct women's conferences and minister to those desiring to grow in Christ, becoming leaders for him in their own countries. Another drastic change has been in the growth of my faith. In the first year of ministry, the cost was approximately $3,000 per conference for a team. It was (all I could do) stretching to trust God for that amount. Today, that same amount is not enough to pay for one team member to go. But God remains faithful. When he gives the assignment, he meets me in my faith, and the supply is met.

Since 1996, WWAM has been instrumental in training thousands of women in over forty nations for leadership among their people in establishing God's kingdom on earth, with our emphasis on India, the Philippines, and Sri Lanka. Our teams train, equip, and educate women leaders in the foundations of the Word, as well as the present truth, apostolic revelation coming forth from the Word. Our teams also conduct pastors' conferences for the release of his glory upon the earth. Having found our place in Christ Jesus, we experience incredible authority and power as we are led by the Spirit.

As women who understand that we were called before the foundation of the world and have been given a clear vision of our divine assignments, we move out in confidence to accomplish those assignments. There we find joy, satisfaction, and a sense of purpose and identity. We do this all for the purpose of bringing in the end-time harvest. God's timing is perfect.

Shift and Divine Alignment

As the years passed, I noticed that the WWAM ministry was becoming one of power with signs and wonders, healings, casting out of demons, and other power demonstrations. Our mindset of traditions has changed, and we are experiencing great authority over the powers of darkness. We have been releasing both men and women to walk in their callings and destiny, also. And as ministry opportunities increase, God is teaching us to work together as a team and not depend on me as the only leader.

The core team members and I were once like butterflies coming forth from our chrysalises. We knew God was up to something new. We didn't know what it would look like, but we continued to press into the call and presence of God. We realized we were in transition. During the long days and nights of wondering what God was up to, we struggled to stay faithful to the call as the battle seemed like an endless tunnel. Now we are apostolic teams going to the nations. God has increased in us, and we are operating in a higher grace, spiritual power, and authority than before.

In the beginning of the season change, I was traveling from South Africa to Chennai, India, passing through Singapore, where I would spend the night waiting for my India team to come from the United States. In search of a room for the night, I called an American woman who had been pastoring in Singapore for twenty-five years. She graciously recommended a very reasonable hotel, and then she invited Janet and me to her church to meet with her for a few minutes. Those few minutes with this amazing woman forever impacted my life.

My friendship and partnership with Dr. Naomi Dowdy benefited me greatly, personally as well as in ministry. She encouraged me in so many new ways. Being a part of her apostolic network gave me a covering and anointing to the ministry that started at the head and has come down upon the body (Ps. 133). The blessing for me has been one of the greatest alignments of my entire life. She has remained my faithful mentor for over twenty years.

Dr. Naomi often spoke of "divine alignments for divine assignments." Her words have proven true for me. Only when the timing was proper did God make this divine connection happen. Perhaps I thought I was ready to meet such a mentor earlier in my life, but he knows who and when to bring together for his purposes on this earth (Rom. 8:28). God's timing is perfect.

As I had a desire and believed I had a call to a certain nation, I often tried over the years to make the connections to make it happen. In frustration, I would cry out to God about it, and he would show me that his ways are higher. The principle he has impressed upon me over and over is to let him make the connections, and do what he calls us to do in his timing. His way leaves no bitter aftertaste. He is the master planner. He knows how to orchestrate for the effectiveness of his people. God's timing is perfect.

Change is not easy, but God remains faithful. In 2014, my husband and life partner in ministry passed. Although I miss him every day, I am moving ahead, by God's grace and strength, into the fullness of time. Once again, new life is beginning to come forth for the new season God has ordained for me and for WWAM.

Birth to Eternity

Because He Said . . .

"For you, O God, have heard my vows; you have given me the heritage of those who fear Your name." (Ps. 61:5, NKJV)

* * *

Our heritage is godly and secure in Christ Jesus. Our heavenly Father is (all) about family. He blesses generationally through our heritage as his children. Our prayers as his daughters and sons never leave the realm of his love and provision, regardless of our human condition. His offers are astounding. We are family. Therefore, in Christ, we, too, can expect an enduring, blessed inheritance. Heritage (has to do with) is based on a set foundation that becomes a springboard for the future.

What was revealed thousands of years ago was a mystery to me. God came to a clueless young woman and made himself known. I am forever thankful for his willingness to welcome the insignificant and overlooked ones, restoring us into his family, the kingdom of God, as his dear children.

How does spiritual inheritance play a role in our lives? I know I have an inheritance and legacy, as all those who enter God's saving mercy and grace. Also, I have had the privilege of being welcomed into the family-line heritage of several godly people in my past.

Slipping Down God's Slide

My childhood didn't include anything about God, heaven, Jesus, or the Holy Spirit. I wasn't sure why Christmas and Easter were celebrated.

Married at nineteen, I began attending my husband Tom's family's church. It was a strange but friendly experience. After a few visits, I wondered if I was being exposed to some weird kind of mind-altering manipulation. I wasn't depressed or sad before I came into the service each Sunday. But by the time we walked out the door, something internally had been altered. I wanted to twirl, skip or dance, and sing all the way home. I felt vastly different Sunday after Sunday but didn't have a clue why. I rarely understood more than a sentence of the preaching. Nevertheless, somehow the morning made me feel warm inside.

Tom didn't realize my pleasure in attending wasn't because I was born from above. I didn't disagree, so he thought it must mean I had experienced the exchange life Jesus offers.

I was painfully shy in those days. I avoided being noticed because my face would glow bright red in embarrassment when people talked to me. I preferred fading into any setting, not only at church. Was it because I was so tall growing up? Was it my freckles, bright red hair, or being called Red?

One Sunday, the preacher lovingly invited anyone who wanted to give their lives to Jesus to come to the front. I longed to answer his invitation but still didn't understand. Fearful thoughts over-whelmed my emotions and created confusion. I was hoping desperately that I wouldn't be embarrassed if I went forward for prayer.

What should I do? Does the God that pastor is talking about really want me? Why? I am a little nobody. I am only a young wife and mother.

What if I start walking down the aisle, and he isn't inviting people like me?

What if I make a fool of myself walking up there?

What if someone asks, "What are you doing?" Or asks me to sit down?

All these thoughts were shouting in my head at the same time (simultaneously).

The congregation was standing, singing "Just as I am without one plea," when the overwhelming, life-changing moment happened. I was pulled literally into the aisle. God's extravagant love gave me a gift by the Holy Spirit's pulling me down the aisle. It was so physical, I thought if I didn't step into the aisle, I would have fallen into it.

My son Cordell is a contractor. I have seen him use a dangerously powerful magnet in his work. That morning in church I pushed against the pull, and the physical drawing pulled me toward the aisle again. After trying to stop two times, I turned to Tom and said, "I need to go forward today for prayer." The pull was stronger than my fear, and down the aisle I went toward a surprised pastor. The Holy Spirit drew me forward, helping me overcome my fears. The next thing I knew, I was saying the prayer that transformed my life.

Can you imagine feeling rivers of love pouring into your mind and chest? That's the best description of my experience. I went down that aisle one person, and walked back another. No one had to tell me I was or would be different. I knew I was completely transformed.

Everything was about to change, and change fast. I felt like a child who reluctantly climbed a tall ladder onto a twelve-foot slide, peering down (at) the steep gradient. But in a leap of faith, hands in the air, I was thrust downward. My heart was beating fast as I plummeted to the bottom in the thrill of the unknown ahead. To this day, I often refer to my adventures with God as slipping down his slide.

A Heart for Evangelism

I wanted to tell everyone about my transformation. It didn't matter if I had just met them, saw them standing in a store staring at a potential purchase, or had known them for years. I wanted them to know what I had found out. I didn't want them to be clueless like I had been about this wonderful Father God who was willing to show them his profound love. It was never merely a head acceptance of a truth I had heard or read in a book. It was a profound inward transformation emerging into a relationship with a living God, Jesus Christ, by the influence and power of the Holy Spirit.

I don't have stories of deep darkness, horrible abuse, overt sin, or rejection before I gave my life to Jesus. The day I surrendered, I had more than I ever dreamed life would offer. My husband loved me; we had a home; I had a new baby girl, Vanessa; and I was surrounded by caring family. I couldn't imagine life better than it was. Yet, though difficult to explain how or why, the change was dramatically better, inwardly and outwardly.

My want-tos changed. I took classes and read the Bible. My passion grew stronger and stronger for people to discover the amazing truth I had been drawn into by the all-encompassing goodness of a loving God. He read my heart, not my head. He led me into a greater purpose for my life when I didn't know there was one.

You would think such a dramatic experience would remove all my fears, following such a loving, gracious God. But it did not. Despite all the wonder and delight, at times my lack of self-confidence and my sense of being incapable would cause a knot of fear in my midsection.

When I first received God's invitations to step up and out in sharing his love, the sense of inability or unworthiness shouted at me. When I first gave my life to Jesus, I believe I was delivered of a demonic spirit of fear. I needed to stop believing my self-disqualifications, so I could hold onto the enablement he had provided so generously.

My life had been punctuated with red-faced, painful shyness over the smallest things. In my first years as a Christian, I had to tackle my lack of knowledge, realizing I was completely ignorant of the Bible or anything related to God. Thank God he didn't leave me there. I must have asked a million questions. Everyone was extremely patient. No one caused me to feel awkward or ashamed when I was ignorant about church etiquette or answers to questions they must have considered obvious.

Strong yearnings began to surface. I couldn't escape a compelling desire to help people know this wonderful Jesus I had met. How would I ever learn enough?

The Missing Piece

It started with the invitation to help in children's ministry at Sunday school a month after my born-again experience. I thought they wanted me to pass out papers or pencils to the children or play a game with them. But no. They were asking me to assist teaching a class. How in the world would I do that? I didn't know anything.

I had no idea how this one invitation would lead to teaching not only children, but teenagers and adults. Again, I felt overwhelmed. *They don't know me, or they wouldn't be asking. I'm new; I haven't even read the entire Bible. What could I tell the children?*

God had a plan. The wise leaders had a plan.

My sister-in-law Carole's patient mentoring gave me strength to keep trying. She was instructive, encouraging, and filled with faith for my involvement to become life-changing. My journey became one of continual growth in understanding Father God's nature and ways. Over time, I sensed his presence enabling me to do what I never thought I could have done.

I am grateful his enablement is stronger than my sense of self-disqualification. One day when I was praying about an invitation, these words came to mind.

Who, me?
Yes, you.
Why me?
I said.
What for?
He bore.
How can?
I AM!

I knew "He bore" meant Jesus on the cross, making a way. "I AM" meant all I needed was God Himself.

It felt like an internal puzzle piece fell into place. Often I acted on the biblical commission "Go and make disciples." Or I was following a strong desire to see people ascertain what I had discovered about the glorious, radical, transforming nature of Father God. After all, Jesus said, "Follow me." Yes, they heard his invitation, but to where? To do what? For how long? So many questions that didn't have immediate answers could have stopped them from following him. Me, too.

What I didn't know then was that my personal family line had inheritance promises that could pass down through the years to me—until two significant events changed my perspective.

The Promise of Heritage

It was my twentieth trip speaking at evangelism and conference settings in the Philippines. I led a multicultural, multinational team working with Aglow International's national president, Teresita Felicio.

As we were packing for the trip, she asked us to bring clothing representing our personal heritage or country of residence. The team was beautifully diverse, and I knew it was a fun idea. But I was not sure how it would be used.

Quality teaching, worship, and healing flowed throughout the days. The team and conference attendees felt like overstuffed chairs bulging at the seams from all the input. We poured out our hearts in passionate messages. Life-giving miracles flowed from testimonies in a simple yet profound demonstration of the love of God. On the last night, we were asked to dress in our international regalia. What was the leader up to? Did the Holy Spirit have something tucked up his sleeve none of us had considered?

Our final evening together was in the making. On the resort's vast lime green lawns, resort workers were stacking white plastic chairs alongside folded tables for the celebratory setup that evening.

Norwegian in family heritage, I had purchased an outfit from Solvang, California, the nearest Scandinavian-heritage town to my home. I added a few touches with ruffled socks and braided my red hair with little bows dangling from the ends.

Teresita said, "Janet, tonight we are going to have a multi-table, orchid-laden buffet filled with local foods set up around the pool. A live worship band will play international celebration songs. We would like you to be the speaker."

It was an honor to be asked. The team had spent four days sharing their hearts. My first concern was how many times our audiences had listened to a speaker from morning to night, day after day. How much more could their minds absorb without feeling overloaded and exhausted?

"What do you think about a different presentation?" I asked. "Instead of my sharing a message, may I ask the multicultural team members to share their personal testimonies of God's goodness as they walk from table to table? Each team member could walk up to a different table one at a time while the guests are dining, introduce themselves, and share the adventures of God's dramatic intervention in their personal lives. Then we would move from table to table around the pool area."

Teresita was delighted. "Yes, that sounds wonderful and interesting. Let's do it."

The musicians softly played a myriad of cultural music praising God in the background punctuated with singers worshiping in their languages as we all took our places at the elegantly decorated tables around the expansive, inviting pool at the resort. The light tropical breeze and setting sun brought a restful, calming effect. As the darkness began to fall, it turned into another gift from heaven as I gazed at the twinkling lights around the pool, orchids adorning the delicious food on the tables, and talkative, shining faces.

It was striking eye candy as the team entered the venue, causing the extravagant lavender and pink orchid arrangements to seem average in comparison. My team was dressed in American red, white, and blue; Chinese silky red; Irish lime; India's gold and white; Filipinos in a variety of colors and designs; and our young male team member in a Jamaican basketball jersey. I felt a bit out of place in my ruffled socks and Scandinavian dress, but it was fun. The African dresses were bold yellow, red, and deep purples, sitting next to brightly colored Japanese kimonos. The dinner guests represented different continents, cities, villages, and tribes.

As the dinner was served, we approached one table at a time, told our transformative story, and moved to another table until we had shared our spiritual jouneys with everyone on the lawn.

I introduced myself with my birth name, Melonie Janet Floen, who became Janet Button, and after marriage, Melonie Janet Mangum. I told my childhood story of never knowing my birth father until I was an adult. I spoke of Darrel, my faithful stepfather, as the one who raised me.

"In fifth grade, my parents and I were in a car accident. They were badly injured in the collision. Relatives were notified. That's how I found out my loving stepfather was not my birth father. As

I look back, I realize I wasn't hurt or devastated by the news, but only curious about who my birth father was. Life went on as usual. Nothing changed with my new awareness of a stepfather as well as a birth father, until after I was married and expecting our first child."

A few letters had passed back and forth between my birth father and me, so I arranged to meet him and his family. The days visiting them were filled with light conversation and storytelling while browsing through old worn photo albums.

What did all this have to do with heritage? Did it have anything to do with becoming a follower of Jesus? What did it have to do with a celebration around a pool in Asia?

After years of compiling experiences, I had a part in leading hundreds and then thousands to a personal relationship with Jesus Christ as their Savior and Lord. I came alongside ministries, helping plant churches in various countries, and had seen thousands of miracles, innumerable healings, and transforming deliverances. I served as head of women's, children's, and youth ministries. I had served as an associate pastor twice and interim senior pastor in churches. Overseas invitations had taken me to over thirty-six countries—twenty-five or more times in one, and several missions in others. This was my normal experience for years, before walking from table to table, sharing my life journeys at the celebration.

A few months before I went to the Philippines on that trip, I received a homemade book in the mail. It was a history of the Floen family on my birth father's side. The pictures were of men and women who traveled from Norway to be missionaries in America long before his birth. I looked at their roles—pastors, leaders, missionaries, and church planters. These were my grandparents and great-grandparents. I was overwhelmed by reading the heritage of a father I never knew who didn't seem to carry on the legacy.

Against the backdrop of the tropical beauty of the celebration event, I continued my story. From the absence of any understanding of God or Jesus to the experiences I had been privileged to taste throughout the years, I had a stunning, internal, aha moment.

I was living out a heritage.

I was the result of prayers from many years ago, for family to come and know Jesus as their personal Savior and Lord. It was a shocking revelation of purpose, plan, and passion. I had inherited it, and God had included my life experiences in that heritage. Who knows how much God added that pertained to just little ole me along the way?

When I returned home from the trip, I searched for the genealogy book again. One old, small Minnesota church with a white steeple was in the pictures. Penciled above one of the pictures were the words, "This was my home church." I googled the address, and it still exists. One day I will have to visit. Who knew God's plan to reveal the heritage he had given long before my birth? Not me.

You, Too

Your earthly heritage may not have the generational believers
we have. It may not be packed with the prayers of your
forefathers. But through your adoption into God's family, the
men and women in the Bible have become your personal
relatives. God brought us into his bloodline prayers of your
biblical family as your personal heritage, and it is part of your
legacy as well.

*"Thy testimonies have I taken as an heritage for ever: for they are
the rejoicing of my heart." (Ps. 119:111, KJV)*

*"But as many as received Him, to them He gave the right to
become children of God, to those who believe in His name."
(John 1:12, NKJV)*

* * *

Can you recall a time in your life when your time frame was
not God's? What was the result? What are the visions or
promises in your life that have yet to be fulfilled? What do you
see as hindrances of these promises coming to pass? Is there a
time when you feel you failed God?

Obedience to the Holy Spirit's leading is imperative. Watch
the Holy Spirit bring an upshift that unveils and identifies his
identity within your own. Step up into the truth of his Word
for your life. Step out into his faith for who you are becoming
in him. Watch God unveil and identify his identity within
your own as you experience his adventures in ways you never
dreamed you could accomplish.

*Holy Spirit, I thank you that you are leading and guiding me into
a royally designed legacy in Christ.*

I Will Make You Fishers of Men

Because He Said . . .

"Then He said to them, 'Follow Me, and I will make you fishers of men.'" (Matt. 4:19, NKJV)

* * *

Who knew that in 1990, I would be in the Philippine Islands with my father, brother, and sister, going village to village telling stories of the Good News? It was like a dream.

I was in the province of Pangasinan on the island of Luzon, riding on the back of a small motorbike with a local pastor driving. We were bouncing up and down, side to side on a hard, dusty road, navigating large rocks along the way. Behind us was a motorized bike with a sidecar carrying two young people who were part of our team. After an hour, which seemed like an eternity with my masked face, dust-covered hair, and long skirt flapping in the wind, we finally reached our destination, a quaint fishing village on the China Sea.

Obviously, the area was very poor. The people's clothing looked worn and dirty, and both adults and children were unkempt. It seemed as though nearly everyone was sitting around their small nipa huts smoking, playing cards, and drinking something unidentifiable.

We were not welcomed. We walked toward the people, but

they simply continued their activities. I thought, *They do not know what to do with us.* The atmosphere was somber with few smiling. This was unusual for Filipinos, typically friendly and hospitable.

Having had little experience in missions at that time, I needed to depend on the Holy Spirit. I knew we must accomplish our mission.

Trusting God

As one of our companions took out his guitar and began singing children's songs, the kids came running to join in. Their big brown eyes danced with delight as the team performed for them. Two of our youth pantomimed a Bible story with a local interpreter. The village children giggled and twirled as they tried to mimic the movements of the actors. The team invited them to become part of the Bible story enactment.

After a small crowd gathered, I began to tell the story of the prodigal son, sometimes acting out parts myself. The ending told God's story of love. We gave an invitation for them to receive Jesus as their Lord and Savior, and the Holy Spirit to come and live in them. We had success with the children. However, the adults were not impressed. They did not come to our little play or appear interested in what we were doing.

I noticed that several people were talking to one man nearby. Then I remembered that small neighborhoods in the islands have a political leader called a "Barangay Captain." This man represented the people and made decisions for the neighborhood. He would be a man of great influence and was either revered or feared.

I was standing before an entire village, an American woman who knew little about the culture. Certainly, they had no idea why I was there. Then an idea struck me. I walked over and greeted the man whom I thought was in charge. Looking at his ragged white T-shirt and baggy black shorts, I said, "I have come from God to bless your people. I am an American, but I love the Filipinos. May

I pray for you and your people? Is there anything you want me to ask God for you?"

Because I presented myself as a religious woman, I suspected he would ask for something spiritual. How presumptuous of me.

He looked up at me, with a big cigarette hanging out of his mouth. Then he gazed at the ocean, where many small carved-out wooden boats bobbed in the water. "We are hungry, and we have no food or money. We are a fishing village, and we supply fish to the surrounding communities in the area. The ocean has stopped bringing us fish. We cannot buy or barter for other items we need. We are desperate. Can God bring fish?"

Faith arose in me as I replied, "Of course, he can."

Then I looked upward to heaven and reverently cried out to God, asking him to bring fish as a witness to these humble people. "Do a sign and wonder so you will be glorified, and your name will be great in this area."

I boldly asked the man, "If God answers your prayers, will you contact my friends who have a church in the area and let them come to conduct a Bible study? Would you honor God in this way in response to answered prayer?"

He was very eager to say yes. Then we gave him all the information required to set up a Bible study. After a short conversation, I hopped on the back of the bike, and we started for our temporary base.

Fish in Abundance

At that time the Philippine government was facing a serious threat from a communist group known as the New People's Army (NPA), a group engaged in violent acts throughout the islands, in hopes of conducting a coup. In fact, they had beheaded a pastor and put his head on a pole near our base shortly before our arrival. Unknown to me at the time, this small fishing village had experienced threats from the NPA and had paid taxes to them.

As I arrived at the home base, one pastor said to me, "Sister Lana, we are so proud of you for your courage and strong faith. You know none of our pastors would go there because of the NPA."

I thought, *Egad! It would have been nice if someone had told me! God is certainly gracious and completely covered our team.*

The next day the local village people experienced a miracle. Fish came into their area, and as the fishermen went out, they brought in boatloads of fish. And, it did not stop. Within a week the man I had spoken to sent word to our friends, and they were ready to establish a Bible study. Several weeks after I arrived home, I received a letter informing me of the result of our visit. You should have seen this lady, jumping up and down, praising God. He was glorified through it all.

You, Too

God reveals himself in miracles today.

"I am the LORD, *the God of all mankind. Is anything too hard for me?" (Jer. 32:27)*

"Jesus looked at them and said, 'With man this is impossible, but not with God; all things are possible with God.'" (Mark 10:27)

"'If you can?' said Jesus. 'Everything is possible for one who believes.'" (Mark 9:23)

* * *

Have you seen any miracles in your own (personal) life?

Consider believing that God is with you and wants to show himself strong by partnering with you in the miracles of life.

I thank you, Lord, that your plan for my life is to glorify yourself through me. Thank you for calling and empowering me through the Holy Spirit. I do believe nothing is impossible with you.

LAUGHTER LEMONADE

Because He Said . . .

"A joyful heart makes a face cheerful, but a sad heart produces a broken spirit." (Prov. 15:13, CSB)

"All the days of the oppressed are miserable, but a cheerful heart has a continual feast." (Prov. 15:15, CSB)

"A joyful heart is good medicine, but a broken spirit dries up the bones." (Prov. 17:22, CSB)

"The one enthroned in heaven laughs." (Ps. 2:4, CSB)

* * *

Perhaps today you feel like you could use some lighthearted enjoyment due to hard work or frustrating circumstances. In Proverbs, the Bible describes a merry heart as having a continual feast. There are times when desperate pleas or heartbroken tears are appropriate responses. Yet, the value of a merry heart with a good belly laugh can't be overlooked either.

Laughter relaxes the entire body and burns calories. It releases endorphins, the body's natural, feel-good chemical, and promotes an overall sense of well-being. Also, doctors have observed that laughing is good exercise for the lungs, heart, diaphragm, and stomach, improving circulation by clearing toxins from the respiratory system. It protects the heart by improving the function of the blood vessels and increasing blood flow. It is your body's natural antidote for stress, pain, and conflict. Some say nothing works faster or more dependably to bring your mind and body back into a healthy balance than laughter.

Could you imagine yourself standing under a tree, wearing large, comical green sunglasses with stickers on your face, speaking to more than forty pastors in a foreign country? Neither could I, and yet I was on one of my first trips overseas with Lana's ministry, Women With A Mission, when I found myself doing laughter workshops. What was I thinking? Why had I decided to do that? It certainly wasn't my norm. My impression was that the team was packed with mighty women of God who could teach and preach on nearly anything. And I was convinced it was my assignment to make them laugh.

The Value of Laughter

The area was suffering from severe draught in Asia that year. As a result, we fed the attendees for several days. The draught and our willingness to supply food brought hundreds of attendees with their entire families. Were we surprised? Yes. Lana called home, and her husband arranged for more funds to buy large amounts of food for the hungry and discouraged.

I marvel every time I think of the providence of God while on one of Lana's teams. Her trust in the Holy Spirit in my life astounded me and was pivotal to my personal growth in my journey over the years. She knew JoAnne Meckstroth was a leader of leaders and gave her the main auditorium with hundreds of ministry leaders. I sat under an enormous shade tree with the forty-plus pastors. The outdoor breeze was more than welcome as we sat in the shade together.

My first teaching session explained the medical value of laughter. I followed up with Scriptures proving God knew the significance of our times of laughter, especially a good belly roll and deep, over-taking laughter. It's spiritual, emotional, and physical, all wrapped up in one bundle of blessing—our body. Job 8:21 declares, "He will yet fill your mouth with laughter, and your lips with shouting" (ESV).

I took out my props, including large, silly sunglasses; a toy wand; colorful stickers; and bulbous, fluorescent-orange rubber shoes. I began by telling stories of my own journey of being trans-formed from sadness, worry, or depression into relief and laughter. It was a choice—an unlikely choice. Yet the benefits I delightfully received from those times were worth the effort it took.

I shared the seemingly silly ways I tried to think on things that would cause me to grin, laugh out loud, or shout with gusto, such as wearing my bulbous orange shoes or putting stickers on my face. The audience was considering what I was saying, and their faces gave no indication how they were responding to a totally different mindset.

I told them our next session on this beautiful day under the soft breeze and shade of the broad-leafed tree would be sharing clean jokes, and each of them should come prepared to share one.

Break time came. As I approached the large auditorium, JoAnne was summing up her compassionate commissioning with the leaders. As she led in prayer, hundreds fell on their knees, tears splashing on the cement floor in front of them. They were being renewed, refreshed, and released from the bondage of their stresses in ministry and family life during this very difficult time. I could feel the presence of the Holy Spirit filling the room with powerful, restorative blessings. It was a stunning realization of God's heart as JoAnne followed the leading of the Holy Spirit's moving among them. I felt as though I had accidentally entered a private session between them and their God, and I was in awe.

The leaders slowly exited the room in a solemn but peaceful manner. As they walked by, I began to feel so foolish. What had I done? JoAnne was meeting deep emotional needs, targeting their sacrifices and ministry lives in a dynamic and healthy way, and I just talked about laughter in big green sunglasses. However, despite my feelings, it was time to listen to people sharing jokes.

I thought, *I missed it totally. I was so foolish to think that was God. I'm embarrassed, but I need to finish what I started.*

I put on my glasses and the fluorescent-orange rubber shoes and stuck children's stickers on my face. I asked God to forgive and help me with the emotional embarrassment, so I could continue what I began, and leave.

Cultural Humor

I didn't know what to expect when we resumed the session, but I was soon surprised when every pastor came with a joke. As they stood in front to begin their funny stories, I would say, "Wait, I have to do something to get you and the audience ready for your story."

With a grin and every now and then turning to the pastors and giving them a big wink, I stuck funny stickers on their noses or cheeks. Then I ran around them a couple times, tapped them on the head with the wand, and said, "Ready? Now go."

It's difficult to describe the silliness I exhibited as I prepared them to tell their jokes. These grown men served as pastors of churches, and some were overseers of several pastors. And I was tapping them on the head with a little wand, placing stickers on their cheeks, expecting them to go along with me.

At first, they appeared stoic until they opened their mouths to tell their hilarious jokes. The whole group roared in laughter each time. After the first two men stood totally still while I decorated them for their presentations, the others began laughing before the joke began. We were quite a sight. I wonder what someone would have thought if they passed by.

My interpreter decided I was being left out of the fun since their jokes were in their language. So he interpreted each joke into English, so I could laugh with them. Each speaker would tell their joke, and the audience roared in laughter as he interpreted it for me. Jokes in different cultures are difficult to interpret, and most cultures find very different things to be funny. So what is funny and made sense to them was an enigma to me. However, I didn't want to disappoint. So I practiced my "laughter on purpose, rip-roaring, belly-rolling demonstration" I had been doing during my difficult times, whether or not the jokes seemed funny.

Afterward, I felt tired and completely spent. I went over to the children and played with them in my big, funny glasses while feeling despondent, that I had missed the Holy Spirit's leading. Hopefully, I hadn't embarrassed Lana with my workshop.

The Right Joke at the Right Time

Later that day, my interpreter asked to talk with me. He was the vice president of a denomination and had several churches himself. You can imagine what I thought he wanted to talk about.

We sat down and he began speaking in a soft, sober, conversational manner. In his ministry culture, he explained, laughter isn't acceptable in ministry settings. It was considered frivolous for many reasons and disrespectful. At home or with close friends, they would laugh and tell clean jokes, but never in a setting like the one we were in.

Before this conference he had decided to step down from his position. It was too difficult to be in his role and take care of his family during those extremely difficult times. But as he interpreted the sessions, laughing at me in my funny outfit, stickers, shoes, and glasses, as well as at the jokes in the last session, he felt his depression and sense of depressive weightiness lift away. He was both healed and delivered from the emotional bondage that had been too heavy to carry, causing him to feel spiritually drained.

Due to what the Holy Spirit had brought to him during our

times together, he realized he could remain and serve. Then another relief and surprise came—he wanted me to do it again as he gathered another group of leaders to experience freedom and healing resulting from the laughter workshops. I did. We did. But most of all God did.

Comparisons can be a healthy evaluation tool. But they can be severely detrimental to our flowing with the Holy Spirit, also. Thank God for the validation I received that day. It could have been a pivotal time that spoke into my life with negative, destructive damage. Instead, God intervened. The Holy Spirit showed himself strong and met the heartfelt needs of his leaders.

You, Too

Maturing in Christ usually requires times of stretching beyond our comfort zones.

"There is a time for everything, and a season for every activity under the heavens." (Eccles. 3:1)

"He will yet fill your mouth with laughter and your lips with shouts of joy." (Job 8:21)

"The joy of the LORD is your strength." (Neh. 8:10)

* * *

Do you need to forgive yourself today?

You, too, may have experienced times when you wondered if what you said or did was the leading of the Holy Spirit. Like me, you probably haven't had all those times validated as I did in this story, with God's unexpected grace. I often say, "Give it your best shot, prayerfully and obediently." Remain teachable and trusting that God has a plan. If you missed it somehow, he can turn it around for good, and like the old saying, "turn lemons into lemonade."

Thank you, Jesus, for forgiving me. I choose today to forgive myself for anything I have not released to you.

Dreams and Prophecies

Because He Said . . .

"Now there was one, Anna, a prophetess, the daughter of Phanuel, of the tribe of Asher." (Luke 2:36, NKJV)

"Your sons and daughters will prophesy." (Acts 2:17)

"[Philip, the evangelist] had four unmarried daughters who prophesied." (Acts 21:9)

* * *

The Old Testament is filled with prophets who engaged in strange, often bizarre, acts as prophetic signs. The acts were natural, not supernatural, but they had spiritual meanings. For example, when Elisha told King Jehoash to take some arrows and strike the ground (2 Kings 13:18). Or when in Nehemiah 5:13 he said, "I also shook out the folds of my robe and said, 'In this way may God shake out of their house and possessions anyone who does not keep this promise. So may such a person be shaken out and emptied!'"

Many dreams in the Bible also were of a prophetic nature, including Joseph in the Old Testament, Joseph (Jesus' earthly father) in the New Testament, and Pilate's wife. Paul dreamed about going to a man who would call him to "come over to Macedonia and help us" (Acts 16:6-10). Scripture tells us that God often uses dreams.

Job 33:15-16 says, "In a dream, in a vision of the night, when deep sleep falls on people as they slumber in their beds, he may speak in their ears."

Dreams, a prophetic "word" from a fellow believer, acts, and signs are to be examined as messages from the Holy Spirit. It is not uncommon when we travel to other countries to teach and train our teams to experience prophetic dreams. When I am on the receiving end of them, I pay close attention to see what the Spirit is saying—and doing—to guide me in his unfolding plans.

Over a three-year period, from 1997 to 1999, God showed me through a series of acts, signs, dreams, and "words" from other trusted friends that he wanted me to go to a nation I had never visited, and honestly, never wanted to go to for any reason.

A "Chance" Meeting

I had recently moved from Portland, Oregon, to Colorado Springs, Colorado, when I received a phone call from my close friend Lyn, whom I had been missing. She had a surprise for me—she had been asked to conduct a retreat at a local church in Larkspur, a small, lovely town just north of Colorado Springs.

"You know how directionally challenged I am!" she blurted out. "I need you to help me navigate my way around."

I did, indeed. She had traveled to several countries with me. I could recall numerous times when I had to chase her down, get her attention, and help her with directions. Small in stature with unending energy, Lyn is beautiful and precocious. Her joy in any situation has always been needed on missions trips, especially when we endured hardships. One of her traits is the ability to close her eyes and fall asleep within fifteen seconds. An august speaker, she is able to engage her audience. As she teaches, her big blue eyes grow large and sparkle, drawing in her audience as though she were a magnet.

I was delighted to help her get around town. At the end of the retreat, the last place she needed to go was the home of a couple in church leadership who were hosting a celebration gathering. I made a great effort to excuse myself from attending the celebration. However, as the Holy Spirit intended, I was meant to go.

Mary and Terry lived in a magnificent home, hidden from view, on acres of land. It was difficult to find, even with good directions. The main garage housed four vehicles, and another housed ten high-end cars. I spotted a landing strip behind the home. I thanked God for men and women who love and serve him whatever their station in life.

Raised Pentecostal, I was familiar with itinerant missionaries fundraising for their mission. Mary and Terry were hosting a handsome, brilliant man from India named Sam, and they wanted to introduce him to as many people as possible during his visit. He was a humble pastor of a ministry in Southern India, India Gospel League.

His ministry presentation interested me with its focus on rural areas, where three-fourths of the nation lived, most in crushing poverty. In India's remote areas, the people knew little of the civilized world or India's modern cities. Sam explained that this holistic, indigenous ministry led with the gospel. Once a core group of believers was established in a village, India Gospel League could initiate literacy training, address health issues, guide rural development initiatives, and establish schools and care centers for children.

After his formal presentation, the group enjoyed snacks and savory hors d'oeuvres. After a few minutes, I decided to leave. As I was putting on my coat, Sam asked if I was a pastor's wife. I told him I wasn't but added that I was very active at my local church. Then he asked what I did.

"I have been blessed to take teams of women around the world,"

I said. "Our purpose is to train and empower indigenous women to win their nations for God."

He looked at me and asked, "Can you be in India next September?"

Powerful Insights

One year prior to that evening, while living in Portland, I had spent a few days with a friend in the mountains to pray and rest. During our morning prayer time we used *The 10/40 Prayer Guide*, initially published by Christian mission strategist Luis Bush. The prayer strategy included praying for every nation inside a large, rectangular geographical area where the majority of the population had little or no knowledge of the gospel of Jesus Christ. The area was known as the 10/40 Window, (lying) across Africa and Asia, between 10 degrees and 40 degrees latitude north of the equator.

One morning, India was the prayer assignment for the day. As Barbara and I prayed, an unusual phenomenon appeared. We were in front of a large picture window facing Mount Hood in all its beauty. In the light blue sky several large clouds drifted. One cloud came down on top of Mount Hood and covered the peak. After a few seconds, the cloud began shrinking and formed what looked like a thin hoop with the mountain top peeking out in the center. The hoop began to move slowly around the mountain, similar to a turning Hula-Hoop.

Excitedly, Barbara said, "I think this is a prophetic sign that you will go all over India training women."

I said I would gladly do it, but that I did not know anybody in India or any ministry there. But I hid the words in my heart.

Several months later, prophetic friend Cheri called to share a dream she had about me. In her dream she was positioned far above a scene, looking down. She saw a huge green forest growing over and covering a dirt road coming out of each side of the forest. I was standing on the right side of the forest, in the middle of the road, looking intently at the entrance to the forest. She saw a man come out of the forest and begin talking with me, trying to convince me to join him in the forest. I appeared hesitant, but the man convinced me to enter with him. Cheri was able to see where we were inside the forest because the leaves on each tree shook as we passed by. We came out of the forest on the left side. She was shocked because thousands of women followed us when the man and I came out.

Then Cheri described the man. He was not very tall, dark skinned but not black, well dressed, and wore glasses. I wrote down her "word," or dream, and put it in my personal file.

One year later I went to the Larkspur meeting and met Sam.

Taken aback by his request to go to India, I said, "Let's stay in touch, send each other materials about our ministries, and we'll see what God will do."

I did not hear from Sam again until May 1999, eight months later. His call came on a Wednesday night. He asked if I remembered him. He wanted to confirm our plan for me to be in India in September. I told him I was leaving for Malaysia within six weeks, and that my team did not yet have the finances for the trip. Then I inquired about the budget for his trip. He said we would partner in the expenses, but he would need $6,000 to begin preparations. I needed to tell him it would be impossible for us to raise funds for India.

Sam said his schedule was packed, but he would call the following Monday. In the meantime, he asked me to pray about going to India. He said his team and God had impressed on him that it was time to thrust women into ministry. I agreed to pray.

As I was going to bed that night, I realized I did not have his phone number. Actually, I knew nothing of his ministry, had no references to contact, nor could I remember the name of the couple who invited me to their home in Larkspur. After discussing it with my husband, John, we agreed that the timing was off. There would be no India ministry.

Confirmation

That night, I had a dream. My bedroom was downstairs on the main level of our house, and our office was upstairs. In the dream, I saw myself hurrying up to the office. Opening my filing cabinet, I pulled out a file on the Larkspur meeting. The invitation to the meeting with Mary and Terry's names and a phone number to RSVP was in the file.

Early the next morning, I ran upstairs, opened the cabinet, and discovered the file. The invitation to the celebration gathering was in it—and I didn't remember receiving it.

I called Mary, the hostess of the Larkspur meeting, to discuss Sam. She gave me the contact information for a woman who knew him well. With great enthusiasm, I called her, and she could not say enough marvelous things, confirming the integrity of Sam and his ministry.

On Saturday morning, I received two phone calls. One was from Lydia, a woman I had trained in intercessory prayer many years before. While presiding over a prayer conference, she mentioned that a woman in Oregon had taught her to pray. Dona, a woman in the audience who was involved in missions, spoke to her and mentioned she, too, had a friend in Oregon. Seeing the Holy Spirit's direction, they both discovered their friend was the same person—me!

Lydia asked if Dona knew how to contact me, and she gave Lydia my contact information. When Lydia called me, we talked for nearly an hour. She said she was happy to locate me, because she had recently dreamt about me. She saw me in India, working with a large ministry, training women. She saw several large crowds of women. The poverty and need were great, but as the women with me began to minister and pray over them, the women were transformed.

Miracle upon miracle was happening. The second call I received was from my dear friend of forty years, Mary, who said she was perplexed. She rarely had dreams, but she dreamt about me the night before. In the dream, I was walking down a very dusty road with fire coming out of my stomach. Hundreds of people were walking to and fro, but none seemed to see the fire except her. Even I was unconcerned. I was walking up to women of all stations of life, some with beautiful saris and dresses, others wearing rags, mostly unkempt, and with matted, filthy hair. Then the dream ended. Mary was puzzled as to its meaning.

How much confirmation does one need? I knew I was headed to India. Now to convince my husband and procure the money.

The Lord Provides

John was very reluctant to finance this trip; we knew almost nothing about the ministry in India. However, he agreed to match whatever God provided over the weekend. On Friday night, I wrote every Christian relative I had to share the project and ask for money. Also, I contacted all my close friends, explaining the miracle of the call, asking for their support.

I was extremely disappointed when no one answered my plea.

As I attended church Sunday morning, I was confident someone would come up to me and give me money. I had already received confirmation that I was going to India. I was disappointed when no one gave me money in either the Sunday morning or evening service. I slept fitfully that night.

I expected a call from Sam on Monday morning, but it did not come. Close to noon, I got a phone call from two women who had been missionaries in the Philippines for years. They lived in Redding, California, and had played an important role in my first few mission trips. They knew how to hear God.

"What in the world is going on with you?" they asked.

"What did you mean?" I replied.

"Last night the Holy Spirit impressed on us to each send you $500."

These were single, older women who lived on a very tight budget. I was flabbergasted. I started crying as I told them about the trip to India. I had my "seed."

After lunch I picked up my mail, and a check for $1,000 from a couple who had never given to the ministry was there. And they have never given since. Also in the mail were several small checks adding up to $1,000. I had $3,000!

When John and I were eating dinner that night, he looked across the table at me, almost smiling, and asked, "Well, did God give you the money?"

"He did," I replied.

He looked totally surprised. "Where did you get $6,000?"

I told him about receiving the $3,000, and with his matching funds offer, I had the money."

John smiled with a twinkle in his eye. "Yes, you do."

Sam called that Monday evening. He apologized for not calling sooner, but Ohio had the worst snowstorm in its history that day, and his plane could not land as planned. He traveled all day to get to Los Angeles, where he was waiting to board a plane to return to India.

"Any chance you will be in India in September?" he asked.

I answered confidently, "Yes, we will be there."

Through the listening and obedience of a handful of women to the Holy Spirit's promptings, a movement to transform the women of another nation was about to be born.

You, Too

The Holy Spirit opens doors that no man can close.

"These are the words of him who is holy and true, who holds the key of David. What he opens no one can shut, and what he shuts no one can open." (Rev. 3:7)

* * *

What would have happened if I had not gone to that meeting in Larkspur that evening? Do you have a story regarding divine appointments, and how God led you?

When God arranges holy appointments for us, he doesn't usually explain them in advance. But we can remain confident in their outcomes for the kingdom. And in turn, we learn more about our heavenly Father with each connection he makes for us.

Holy Spirit, in Colossians 4:3, Paul asks the people of Colosse to pray that God would open a door for his message. Therefore, I, too, ask you, Holy Spirit, to open the doors for me so that I may proclaim the mystery of Christ.

Pivotal Connections

Because He Said . . .

"He has made everything beautiful in its time. He has also set eternity in the human heart; yet no one can fathom what God has done from beginning to end." (Eccles. 3:11)

"As it is written: 'The one who gathered much did not have too much, and the one who gathered little did not have too little.'" (2 Cor. 8:15)

"Be strong and courageous. Do not be afraid or terrified because of them, for the LORD your God goes with you; he will never leave you nor forsake you." (Deut. 31:6)

*   *   *

I cannot count the times I have felt that my contribution in prayer or speaking wasn't good enough. My self-evaluation fueled from discouraging opinions could have ambushed my role in God's strategies for my life.

In my first baby steps as a Christian, I was encircled by a church family who both challenged and encouraged me with training, wisdom, and support. But a few years later after our move to a new city, I became well acquainted with the pain of disqualification. Was I enough? Would I ever be enough? Healthy growth in character and skills requires honest evaluations. At times, it was a relief to acknowledge I wasn't quite up to the task. But if I had listened to my inner or outer evaluations of skills, intelligence, or spiritual acuity, disqualification would have reigned.

I am extremely thankful to Susan Ashton, who recorded "A Rose Is a Rose" (available on iTunes and YouTube), a timely gift during my identity struggles. My aching heart absorbed its encouragement when my dreams were being bombarded. Here is just a part of this beautiful message that spoke to me.

> Just keep your heart steady as she goes
> And let them call you what they will . . .
> A rose by any name is still a rose

What was it about me that seemed so different? My enthusiasm wasn't understood. Years later one of the ladies in a Bible study I attended shared with me, "I had to take a tranquilizer every time I knew you would be there. You were too willing to do anything you read in the Bible." It was unnerving for her. For example, the first time I read a book that talked about conversational prayer, I couldn't wait to get to the group and practice. I thought they were going to swallow their tongues at my suggestion.

Eventually, I concluded that I didn't need to know everything or be the best speaker, teacher, or writer. My enthusiastic willingness became an asset. Trust was breeding conviction in the core of my decision-making. It began enabling me to speak up, step out, and watch God. The Holy Spirit astounded me by filling the gaps in presentations. Passion had apprehended my soul, and there was no turning back.

At first it seemed preposterous that I would be afforded the honor of my words changing mindsets. But I couldn't deny I was being compelled to reach for the goodness of God to be revealed in those who desperately needed his intervention. God had engrafted a deep desire to speak into their hearts where he set eternity (Eccles. 3:11). I needed to try.

The discouraging words, intended to stop me, evolved into training grounds. Looking back, I am thankful for the rejections and negative comments I waded through to find myself enjoying the splendid beauty in Christ I was afforded. Those times are no longer gray, depressing thoughts, but sparkling, eternal jewels solidifying my identity in Christ Jesus my Lord. In time, the Holy Spirit sent several pivotal people into my life that drew me into a destiny far beyond my ability to dream up.

A Sister in Christ

Meeting Lana Heightley was the Holy Spirit's designated opportunity, becoming pivotal for the rest of my life. Lana was the speaker at an Aglow International women's event. My mouth dropped open in amazement when she shared her testimony of the Holy Spirit's notable miracles of salvations and healings in the Philippines. Here in my city, sitting at my table, chatting casually, was a woman who lived a level of dynamic works of God. I was overwhelmed with awe. I had never met anyone who experienced this level of Christianity. I was bursting to ask her a myriad of questions, but too shy to do so.

My good friend Dona and I have birthdays one day apart. What do you do to celebrate each other when your friend's birthday is so close? "I will take you to lunch." "No, I will take you." "Let's forget it, go to lunch, and each pay." We had decided that year would be different. We would find somewhere to go together to celebrate our birthdays. Where could we go? What would we do?

Browsing through *Charisma* magazine, my eyes fell on a Women in Ministry conference in Oregon. It sounded like a good idea.

"What do you think, Dona?"

"Good idea."

"Do you remember Lana Heightley?"

"Of course. She was that powerful woman of God who spoke a couple years back."

"She lives in Oregon now. Give her a call, and see what she thinks of the conference."

Sure enough, Lana not only gave the conference a thumbs-up, she also invited us to stay with her instead of at a hotel. As I was prayerfully packing, I heard a whisper in my soul, *Ask her to pray for you for how you do missions.* It was an odd thought, since I didn't see myself as "doing missions."

When we arrived at her house, I was uncomfortable telling her what I had heard from the Holy Spirit. My recent attempts to volunteer for missions work had been met with squinty-eyed skepticism. I didn't want to seem presumptuous. How would she react? Finally, I got the nerve to ask, haltingly, "Lana, would you pray for me for how I do missions? You don't have to prophesy to me; any simple prayer will do."

"Of course. It would be my pleasure. Let me pray about it first."

The conference was filled with women employed by a church to lead their women's ministry. That wasn't Dona and me, but we were challenged with the teaching and had a good time together.

The conference concluded with Lana's offer to treat us to an elegant dinner overlooking the river. As we sat at the table enjoying delicious food, Dona and Lana began telling their stories. Lana looked thoughtfully at my wide-eyed enjoyment of their chatter. "Janet, usually I wouldn't tell these stories in front of someone like you who hasn't traveled much. I believe you are about to start traveling in ministry. I hear the voice of the Spirit saying to you, *Pack your bags.*"

In that moment, I grabbed hold of all the courage I could muster and asked softly and haltingly, "If my name ever comes to mind when you are forming a team, I would love to go."

Her affirming response was the opposite of any I had heard previously. "You would always be welcome, but I almost died on my last trip. I'm taking some time before I go again."

The evening continued with good food and conversation; it was as if the whole room was transported to another location, and there we sat, the three of us. The thick, tangible presence of God felt like an invisible, immense bubble surrounding our table. My awareness of the Holy Spirit was so poignant I couldn't make a sound for several minutes. I sat there awestruck.

Lana broke the silence with an exuberant declaration: "I know what I am supposed to do. I will offer leadership training for the women in developing countries." She turned to Dona and me. "Yes, please come and be a speaker on my team."

Lana's Asian team invitation was a shock. She had never heard me teach. Why would she offer me an invitation? Would I be able to fulfill her expectations? How about God's? Maybe I should decline with gratitude for being asked. In that brief encounter, being asked felt more than enough.

It was too intriguing to back out now. The truth was I didn't want to back out. Everything within me wanted to taste and see what could happen when I said yes.

Trusting God

What I didn't know about ministry in general or the Filipino culture was immense. But it was to be a pivotal, impacting, empowering, and completely mind-blowing experience that would transform the rest of my life.

Did it take courage? Sure, it did. Lots of it. I had to find a way to raise the extra money and develop messages for a new culture and setting. We were going to the Philippines. I didn't even know what a Filipino looked like. I felt silly asking people if they knew a Filipino. I researched online and in churches. It was an incredible stretch to believe the Holy Spirit would lead and empower me on such a venture. Yet, he gave me enough faith to trust and keep moving forward. Like my salvation experience, it was a magnetic pull from the Holy Spirit that kept drawing me toward this transitional adventure.

Excitement before our arrival became exhaustion, with the multiple hours of travel and fatiguing jet lag, and no day to rest. We arrived, unpacked, ate a bite, and climbed into the back of the jeepney heading for the event site. As we approached a mall parking lot filled with small plastic chairs instead of cars, I was stunned, being outdoors with hundreds of attendees seated and waiting.

The introductions were brief. Worship blasted from enormous stacks of speakers vibrating across the vast parking lot. I was the first speaker after worship. The team of women prayed for me, promising to cheer me on as I spoke. Talk about needing courage. As I stood, I wondered what in the world I said yes for. The women didn't know me. I didn't know the culture. And a translator was standing beside me, waiting for me to begin.

As I started my message, I looked at the team seated in the front row for encouragement. They were exhausted, their heads bobbing downward, their eyes uncontrollably crossing or closing. Their desire to encourage me was real, but their ability to stay awake was unrealistic. The women would shake themselves every now and then, trying to wake up.

Great! Big help, gals! I thought. It was time to ignore them, look out at the grinning faces, and take a big breath, trusting God with all that was in me.

Oops . . .

I had requested that a clear glass bowl of water be set on the speaker's stand next to me. I had brought a cloth visual aid to illustrate transformation, a small washcloth tightly wound into an egg-shaped ball. I began, "The water in the bowl represents the Holy Spirit. The tightly rolled cloth ball represents who we are without him."

I plopped the ball into the bowl of water and continued my message. The water unfolded the ball for everyone to see. Did I return to explain the illustration in my message? No, I forgot it was there.

In the clear bowl, for everyone to observe, was an unwound, colorful illustration of how the Holy Spirit transforms our lives. At least in my mind, that's what it depicted. Not only did I forget the cloth and its purpose, I failed to make the main point of the sermon. Sitting down next to my half-awake teammates, I was thankful to be finished. When I looked up, I saw the unwound cloth floating in the bowl. You can imagine how ridiculous I felt.

What I didn't know at the time is that when a speaker isn't clear in their message, a good interpreter will bring the clarity and purpose into the translation. They fill in the gaps, so the listeners understand. But for God, the Holy Spirit, and the interpreter, my point would have been lost. But inspiration from the Holy Spirit graciously filled our time together. Understanding came. The audience jumped to their feet, celebrating Jesus, alive in their hearts.

Isn't that what the Holy Spirit does for us? We do the best we know how and trust him to fill in our "oops." Isaiah 1:19 and 2 Corinthians 8:15 were a relief for my embarrassed soul that day. To those who have little, he fills the gap. For those who are willing and obedient, they will eat the good of the land. I stepped up, stepped out, and watched God's goodness prevail. Would any one of us want it any other way?

You, Too

Courage is a choice to believe in his love and supernatural ability.

"I eagerly expect and hope that I will in no way be ashamed, but will have sufficient courage so that now as always Christ will be exalted in my body, whether by life or by death."
(Phil. 1:20)

* * *

Have you ever doubted your abilities because someone else doubted you first?

Let go of being disheartened by your own sense or lack of ability. Refuse the invalid thoughts from those who question your potential, your dream, or your possibilities, with a teachable spirit and willingness to learn and grow.
Let the doubters doubt. It doesn't have to stop the courageous. The odds are with you in Jesus your Lord. Worship Father God for the gracious gifts of the Spirit that are far beyond your own ability. You are his rose with the sweet fragrance of Christ.

Holy Spirit, I agree with Romans 8:28, trusting you are causing all things to work together for good in my life. I choose to love God and be called according to his purpose. I believe the Holy Spirit is making me courageous and humble, empowering me to press forward in becoming more like Jesus.

Teaming to Launch a Movement

Because He Said . . .

"When they had done so, they caught such a large number of fish that their nets began to break. So they signaled their partners in the other boat to come and help them, and they came and filled both boats so full that they began to sink." (Luke 5:6-7)

"In addition, some of our women amazed us." (Luke 24:22)

"Then some of our companions went to the tomb and found it just as the women had said." (Luke 24:24)

*   *   *

I love team ministry. Why? First, I think it is biblical, especially in the New Testament. Second, I recognize my limitations in some spiritual gifts and that I need others who are stronger in those gifts than me. My husband, who was a CEO for several technology companies, gave me this insight. His leadership style was to hire people who had strengths he did not have and were better in their areas of expertise than he was. He knew that if they succeeded, he would, too. He was a very secure person who understood who he was and, more importantly, who he wasn't.

When I started taking teams with me, I applied this same principle. I looked for women who were more talented and stronger in the gifts in which I am weak. Over the years, it has proven to be an immensely powerful strategy.

Jesus gathered a team for ministry. Besides choosing twelve men to assist in the spread of the Good News, he had a team of women. He influenced many women. However, he had a personal, close relationship with certain ones. They shared their gifts and resources with him in his ministry, and they supported him financially. A few of them are especially memorable: Mary, his mother; Mary Magdalene, from whom he cast out seven demons; Mary, the mother of James and Josesph; Salome, who brought spices for his burial preparation (thought to be Mary's half sister) and was the mother of James and John; Susanna, who also offered her resources; and Joanna, wife of Chuza, a steward to King Herod Antipas and therefore a valuable companion.

Paul had a team for ministry as well, as did Barnabas and Peter. James, Jesus' brother, besides having a team, established a community of believers in Jerusalem.

Sam Stephens understands and implements the principle of teams in his significant and crucial ministry, India Gospel League, also. It is a holistic ministry whose impact is widened and deepened by teams of indigenous men and women using their gifts to work together in ministry.

It Takes a Team

I met Sam in an unlikely place, Larkspur, Colorado, a year before I sensed God was opening the door for me to go to India. Because Janet and I were using our world tickets to fit in as many trips as possible, we joined our team from America for our first trip to India by flying into Singapore. From there, all of us could fly to India together.

After a restful night at the airport hotel, we set out for Chennai, on the eastern coast of the Indian Ocean in the state of Tamil Nadu. I recall the distinct feeling as our plane began its descent into that nation. It was a dark night, and the low-wattage lights of the city made me uncomfortable. I wondered if we were qualified to minister in such a large place. But as our hosts met us at baggage claim with smiling faces and hopeful eyes, that feeling left.

After a harrowing ten-hour drive to the mission compound, we piled out of the van to see a feast of beauty. Sharon Gardens was breathtaking. The atrium where we would be lodged contained some of the most beautiful flowers I had ever seen. Nestled in wide-ranging shades of green, they were awe-inspiring. And the weather, tropical and warm, was very soothing. Rooms had air conditioning, a joy to all, and the cuisine was delicious.

A meticulously dressed woman who was overjoyed to see us greeted our team. Her face was shining with happiness and anticipation as she cried out, "*This* is my team." That beautiful woman was Prati, the manager of Sharon Gardens, the first lady of the compound, and the wife of Sam. We soon discovered that she is brilliant, a great administrator, and filled with wisdom. Prati would be the chief architect of our stay and activities.

Prior to our visit, Sam and I agreed that he would provide seven women who were competent in the Word, strong in the faith, and steadfast for the kingdom. I would bring seven women also, so that we could work in pairs to train and empower the Indian women for ministry. I laugh now remembering how I thought *we* would be the trainers. It was a partnership; they trained us in ministry as well. I was reminded of the story in Luke 5:6-7 when both parties were enlarged and benefited from each other. Ultimately, that is what happened with Prati's and our teams. It took a team to catch all the fish.

Finding Freedom

It was our first time in India, and we faced many unusual cultural issues. To be trained and empowered, first the women needed to be freed from their oppressions. Everywhere we went, we used all our gifts and resources to do that. Women in India endured oppressions of caste by birth, as well as demonic presences, resulting from animism and the Hindu and tribal practice of worshiping many different gods. Team member Wendi shared one example of the work we were called to in India.

There we were, seven of us, in Salem, India, sweltering hot with beads of salty sweat running down our backs. Women of all ages were present for the National Indian Women With A Mission Conference. I was privileged to be one of the keynote speakers that day. My topic was "Renewing Your Strength in the Presence of God."

By far, it was the most massive crowd I had ever spoken to, and I detected a slight rumble as I stood up to take my place at the podium. I gently surveyed the crowd, appearing as though I were trying to make intimate eye contact with each attending constituent. The auditorium held two thousand, and every chair was occupied by women. It was like looking out into a sea of bright colors; Indian female attire is the most brilliant, beautiful fashion in the world.

Suddenly a warm blanket of hush fell on the room, and all eyes were on me—eyes of women beautifully brown, with welcoming smiles, Bibles opened, and pens in hand. This day had finally come. For them, seven beautiful American women of God had traveled thousands of miles to be with them and teach them the perfect Word of God. For us, it was a privilege beyond words or measure to be revered, honored, and made to feel worthy of their time and week long attention.

I began sharing Scriptures and testimonies on God's power and presence in my life, and his desire to reveal himself to them in a unique way. It was a great pleasure to see all two thousand women engage with me through timely laughter at my dry humor, communicated through a translator. They carefully took notes as I shared the perfect and life-healing presence of God with them. At the end of the twenty-five-minute message, it was time to activate physically what they were learning cognitively about the power and presence of God.

The lights dimmed, and I gave explicit instructions how we were going to invite the Holy Spirit to come and speak to us.

"There are only two rules that need to be present as we're waiting on God at this time," I said as they were preparing their hearts for the unknown. "Rule one, no talking to your neighbor. We don't want to distract anyone who wants to experience God in this way."

"Rule two," I continued. "No praying, only listening to God."

I could tell that this rule sparked a curious hope in many as they were about to encounter a part of God that would change their lives forever. Some would joyfully hear his voice for the first time.

As each woman sank comfortably into a bright orange, bleacher-tiered chair in the covered but open-sided auditorium, the music played softly. There was not a peep in the building. All four thousand eyes seemed to be closed, and the focused, squinting expressions on the faces of the sea of women indicated to me their intense desire to see God, hear God, or at least feel him there with them.

During this time of quiet, we waited for approximately five minutes. Suddenly, at the top tier of the auditorium to my left, I saw a tiny woman, very thin and wrinkled, as if she were one hundred years old, begin to make her way down by the stage. I alerted my team of her activity.

At the same time, I coached the women through their reverent silence before the Lord. As I talked to the crowd, the little "mama" made her way to the altar area of the stage and headed toward the stairs that led up to me.

Lana got up and quietly walked over to see what the aged Indian woman wanted. She was close enough for Lana to know that not only did she have wrinkled, hard-life, aged skin, but she was missing many teeth and wearing old, dirty clothing. Thinking she was only enthusiastic about meeting us, Lana put her hand on the woman's shoulder to ask her lovingly to return to her seat. At that moment of contact, the woman screamed and flailed her arms toward Lana.

She was in a full-blown demonic manifestation on the stage, in front of God and everyone.

Not wanting to draw attention to the commotion, I spoke softly through the microphone over the soothing background music. I assured the women, who were in another dimension with the Lord, that Jesus was in the process of setting this woman free. "This is (part of) what happens when his presence is with us. He heals and sets us free from our hurts and demonic tormentors."

Lana, along with two others on our team, was in the back room of the stage, ministering to the tormented woman. They were binding the evil spirits that had continued to torment her throughout the years. Those of us on stage and some of the audience could hear the screams and several different voices of conflict, along with the firm and authoritative commands from our team for this to go out of her.

After about twenty minutes of corporately tuning out the thrashing sounds in the back, the women in the audience were becoming aware that the session was coming to an end. Many were gently wiping the tears of their loving encounters with God off their beautiful cheeks. The peace of God was evident in the auditorium. At the same time, Lana, the team members, and the little "mama" came out from backstage.

They all looked a bit frazzled, their once perfectly styled hair in a mess, their faces sweaty and smeared. Lana's scarf was torn, and the safety pin that held her scarf in place was broken in half. But the little woman was smiling. Her face glowed with grateful joy and peace. Jesus had set her free from the demonic torment she had experienced for years.

The crowd of women and I broke out into great applause to Jesus for this woman's new freedom. Lana sent "mama" to her seat for the next session. As Lana made her way back, she looked at me, and with her elegant and classy style, she smiled and assured me that the next one was mine.

The Start of a Movement

The seven Indian women we partnered with on that first trip went on to do amazing things. They began conducting small meetings. They established churches and more teams in at least twenty-five states in India. Their voices, along with many others who have joined with them, are being heard. Tens of thousands are being discipled and trained in kingdom values.

God is proving himself strong on their behalf to reach their people. Our twenty-year partnership has helped change the face of India in the rural villages. Schools, churches, towns, businesses, and society have been transformed. The wealthy and privileged, as well as the poor and disenfranchised, have been changed by the gospel message of hope. Women have been lifted out of darkness and brought into the kingdom of light. Many have been trained in business and medicine. Others have received healing, and countless more have been set free from oppression. Most importantly, all have been given hope for a future and destiny.

Other team members have been instrumental in the work taking place in India since that trip. Belinda Kendall has been faithful in her leadership over many years, taking teams to partner with Prati. She is tireless in her acts for God. Many other amazing women have gone with me. I am forever grateful to Pat, Sandy, Cheri, Diana, Sheila, Janet, Sherry, Cherie, Jan, Lyn, Wendi, Debbie H., Carol, Wilma, Betty, Melanie, Catherine, Jessica, Elise, Pam, Lynn, Carol, Kathy, and Debbie S. for their stand, sacrifice, and walk with God in India and its nearby island, Sri Lanka. And, the teams of Prati must be commended. By working together, we launched a movement of God, reaching the entire nation and beyond.

You, Too

God works within alignments. He aligns us with people who are mutually beneficial for the extension of his kingdom.

"Just as a body, though one, has many parts, but all its many parts form one body, so it is with Christ." (1 Cor. 12:12)

* * *

Where is God aligning you? While you cannot know in advance what his plans could be, are you open to his leading?

In the book of 1 Peter it says each of us should use whatever gift we have received as faithful stewards of God's grace in its various forms. God has given you supernatural gifts that only you can bring to the party.

Holy Spirit, show me where I fit in the spiritual house you are building.

FROM DEATH TO LIFE

Because He Said . . .

*"Very truly I tell you, whoever believes in me will do the
works I have been doing, and they will do even greater
things than these, because I am going to the Father. And I
will do whatever you ask in my name, so that the Father
may be glorified in the Son. You may ask me for anything in
my name, and I will do it." (John 14:12-14)*

*"I am the resurrection and the life. The one who believes in
me will live, even though they die; and whoever lives by
believing in me will never die. Do you believe this?"
(John 11:25-26)*

*   *   *

The Victor

Resurrection Sunday 2020 was a strange day. No churches were
open. No corporate church worshiping together. No crowds. No
new, pretty, bright Easter clothing. No family brunch gatherings.
For the first time ever, I was not with my family on Easter Sunday.
The restrictions on my space and movements were unfathomable.
I was sheltering in place.

My thoughts ranged from observing unbelievable circumstances
to knowing that "this too shall pass." Who could have known that
a deadly plague would be on the entire world? For the first time

since Noah, all the nations of the world would be affected simultaneously. And for the first time since the original Passover in Egypt, over 3,300 years ago, the entire Israeli nation would be quarantined in their own homes. Who knew cities would be shut down? Who knew that a time of uncertainty, pain, and turmoil could come so quickly?

A moment of truth came to me. This global health crisis could turn into a more terrifying situation. Tens of thousands could die. And with the ensuing economic ramifications, many would be without money to pay their financial obligations. What about the families who needed groceries or help paying rent? I was overwhelmed. What would happen next?

I longed for the fellowship of the church. Why? Because deep in my being, I knew Jesus, our Savior, was alive. This was his day— the day that changed everything. This day was and is *the* life-giving day. I needed intimate worship with mature saints, and I wanted to be with his church.

His church is not a building or a gathering, but a living organism, and his followers are living stones, being built into a spiritual house (1 Pet. 2:5). We are destined to be and meet together to worship him. Yet in that time of extreme social distancing, I was missing the personal touch and the faces of my family and friends.

Like David, I needed to be encouraged and find strength in the Lord my God (1 Sam. 30:6). I needed to talk to my own soul. I did this by completing my daily morning Bible reading and devotion time. My faith was stretched. Then I joined in with worship music from several online churches. Again, my faith was infused. When I listened to preachers giving Word-filled sermons via Facebook, again my faith was enlarged. Finally, at the culmination of celebrating digitally the glory of Resurrection Day with others, I was praising, clapping, and laughing. And crying as well. My faith had been restored. I had received hope and comfort.

My mind turned to the times Jesus brought hope and comfort

by conquering death, and his resurrection from death to life by God himself. Three times, Jesus reached into death and pulled people out. In one instance, all the death sounds were playing as he entered the home of Jairus, whose daughter had died. I love how Jesus told them to stop wailing. Then he said to the young girl, "My child, get up!" (Luke 8:54). Her spirit returned, and she stood up. What power!

In another instance, Jesus and his disciples entered the city of Nain. At the town gate, the body of a young man was being carried out. How heart-wrenching the scene must have been. The boy's mother was a widow, and she had counted on this son to support her for life, as was the custom. All her hopes for the future were pinned on him, yet he had died.

Jesus' heart was with her in her situation. He said, "Don't cry," and to the youth he commanded, "Young man, I say to you, get up!" (Luke 7:13-14). And he did. Hallelujah!

The third and most spectacular instance is the most famous death story of all. He brought back to life Lazarus, who had been dead and entombed for four days. Before Jesus undertook this miracle, he revealed to Martha that he was the resurrection (John 11:25). Then at the tomb, after facing the crowd, a simple statement culminated the miracle: "Lazarus, come out!" (John 11:43).

Even the naysayers were used in the action. He gave them the task of taking off the grave clothes to release Lazarus. This incident enraged the Pharisees, who by the end of the week were calling for Jesus' death. Jesus conquered death, including his own. He was the victor.

A Modern-Day Resurrection

At one of our team's meetings in Sri Lanka, a woman died.

Our team's partners for these meetings were from south India. After completing a sweet, successful women's conference there, they informed us our next conference would be on nearby Sri Lanka, formerly known as Ceylon. The island had a long and violent history. The Tamils, a people group living on the island, had been brought from India by the English to tend tea farms. After being denied their civil rights for almost 150 years, they took matters into their own hands and rebelled against the Sri Lankan government. Unfortunately, they resorted to committing terroristic acts. The civil war had raged for over thirty years.

After landing in Colombo, the capital of Sri Lanka, we were driven a couple of hours north to Negombo and an open-air, luxury hotel. It was a magnificent building, with grounds located on the beach. We felt as if we were in paradise.

The next morning, we went to the conference meeting place on schedule. It was someone's lush, green personal compound. God's handiwork was on display in the exotic flowers and varied shades of green on tree leaves. Then we saw it. The large, white corrugated metal roof of a structure with open-air sides. Three hundred women sat inside.

At one end was a makeshift stage with bright red and blue material covering the floor and extending to the bare ground. The sign announcing our team was a large banner, in blue and yellow, that read "Choose the Good Portion."

We took our place on the stage, and as was our custom, I asked the women where they lived. Many provinces were represented, but noticeably absent were women from the north. It seemed as if only people from the south of the island came. Unknown to us, the island was divided into north and south because of the war. Heavily guarded checkpoints on highways kept both the northern and the southern people from traveling outside their boundaries. It was a tactic to squelch terrorism.

After the opening service, a woman came to us and said that she was from the north. She was a doctor and because of her education and professional position, she was allowed to leave her area. She shared that her husband had insisted she attend our conference to investigate, but she was not sure why.

The first day of the conference, all went well, with ideal unity. The worshiping and sharing was excellent, with one exception. We needed to employ two interpreters. One translated our English into Tamil, and the other translated Tamil into another island language, Sinhalese. It meant we needed to shorten our messages and be more succinct.

The second day of meetings, God displayed his power through an unexpected, miraculous sign. Sherry, a first-time missions team member, was preaching about God's love. At the same time, the rest of our team was resting under a large shade tree, enjoying cold drinks, listening to the teaching. Suddenly, a woman about two-thirds of the way toward the back of the structure screamed and fell onto the dirt floor. Several women went to her and carried her out of the meeting.

After a few minutes, one of the local leaders rushed over to us and said that the woman had died. In haste, I ran to where she had been taken. She had been laid out under another large tree on the other side of the tent. The woman's face was a bluish color, and her eyes were wide open. The doctor whom we had met the day before was present also. She looked at me, very distressed, and said, "She has died. There is no life."

Another first-time team member, Pat, looked at me, and we knew instantly this was not a permanent death. The Holy Spirit raised up in me, and I commanded, "Spirit of death, take your hands off her. You have no legal right to take her."

I knew the days of her life had been numbered, and that she would not be taken until they were lived out. Then I thought of 1 Corinthians 15:55 and cried out, "Where, O death, is your sting?" Pat made some powerful declarations also.

We both felt holy anger as we realized that Satan, the adversary, was trying to bring death to this wonderful saint and cause a distraction for the meetings. We continued quoting Scriptures about life and the giver of life.

Suddenly, the dead woman made a loud coughing sound, choking up a long, struggling breath, and looked at us, shocked. A resurrection had taken place!

After some medical attention by the doctor, the woman was able to stand and go to her room. That night she was back in our meetings, praising God and rejoicing for her life. Can you visualize the praising and celebration in that service?

Today, when Pat recalls that experience, she says she has not been the same since. "The doctor had become hopeless with the need in her area and church. However, after seeing the dead raised before her eyes, she returned home, encouraged with the goodness and strength of God to continue their mission. Lana and I stood in amazement at how God had worked through those who were willing to step into his grace to love others through him."

One Touch of God

Miracles hinge on our attitude and action. We must give the message of hope of Christ in every situation. He has conquered death, hell, and the grave.

That trip was one of victory in so many ways. Our team had many experiences that reminded us of the book of Acts. The raising up of women in leadership to the nations. An illiterate woman pointing to a place in the Bible and asking people to read it aloud to her, and then witnessing to them about what they had read. She became an evangelist, resulting in hundreds coming to Christ. Our team was blessed to dedicate new churches. And we were able to witness the baptism of thirty new believers in the Indian Ocean before returning home.

Yes, Jesus is alive. No virus, storm of life, or circumstance can change the fact that he is risen. Because he lives, we, too, live and are called to do his mighty works.

You, Too

Spending time in God's Word teaches you his ways.

"As the time when the Jews got relief from their enemies, and as the month when their sorrow was turned into joy and their mourning into a day of celebration. He wrote them to observe the days as days of feasting and joy and giving presents of food to one another and gifts to the poor." (Esther 9:22)

"Yet he has not left himself without testimony: He has shown kindness by giving you rain from heaven and crops in their seasons; he provides you with plenty of food and fills your hearts with joy." (Acts 14:17)

* * *

How often do you face situations where you don't know what to do? Do you spend time in the Word learning God's ways?

As you put God's Word inside of you, the Holy Spirit will lead in ways you never dreamed of. Consider looking for ways to give even the smallest gift to someone in need. Kindness is God's way. Look for ways to emulate him in your daily life.

Lord, you are breathing resurrection life into all things that pertain to life and godliness.

THE RICKETY STAGE

Because He Said . . .

"Therefore, my dear brothers and sisters, stand firm. Let nothing move you. Always give yourselves fully to the work of the Lord, because you know that your labor in the Lord is not in vain." (1 Cor. 15:58)

"Therefore, my brothers and sisters, you whom I love and long for, my joy and crown, stand firm in the Lord in this way, dear friends!" (Phil. 4:1)

*   *   *

Paul wrote not only to servants or people anointed to do a task, but to brothers, sisters, and friends—in other words, family. Our relationship with our heavenly Father, as well as with each other, strengthens our courage when we are far removed from our experience and comfort zone, feeling as if we are falling off a cliff. I have found my dearest friend, Jesus, is there to uphold and transform.

It was my first time in Bohol, Philippines. Pastor Powell Lemons and I led the Malibu Vineyard team. I was thrilled to be a coleader of an evangelism team. My excitement outweighed any fear, reasonable or not.

After morning devotions the trucks were loaded with equipment in preparation for our first evangelistic outreach that evening. I had met Pastor Powell a year earlier when in the Philippines with his sister Lana. As I watched him preach, and the worship team sing their praises throughout the barangay, I was enthralled. I wondered if God would allow me to have a part in an evangelism outreach like this. Was it just a wish, or a Spirit-led reality? I felt like a little girl seeing her first candy store.

At the end of that eventful evening, I approached Powell and asked, "Is it possible that someone like me could do anything like that?"

He answered with an affirming smile, "Would you like to learn?"

"Oh yes" was my eager response.

"I'll teach you. You get the team, and I will train you."

It was unbelievable to my ears. Lana had invited me a year earlier to join her team training female leaders. Now her brother was offering to train me how to do evangelistic outdoor events. I couldn't wait to get started.

On-the-Job Training

Pastor Powell had prepared the team and me, so as novices, we were as prepared as possible. Our arrival was uneventful. However, setting up the home where we would be staying was challenging. How would we divide the women's quarters from the men's? We nailed a rope from wall to wall, and hung a couple sheets over it. Where would I brush my teeth? I ended up standing next to Powell, feeling quite awkward.

He seemed to read my mind. "It's okay, Janet. You can brush your teeth next to me."

Team members' luggage was stacked everywhere, allowing little space for privacy. But we managed to get settled, blow up our air mattresses, and in the midst of the loud snoring, attempted to get a good night's rest.

The tropical setting was perfect for an outdoor breakfast of freshly baked bread, mangoes, and coffee. The Filipinos joined us by leading in worship, prayer, and communion. Then after morning devotions, the trucks were loaded with equipment in preparation for our first evangelistic outreach that evening. We followed later in the day piling into jeepneys, armed with our water bottles, Bibles, and sweat cloths.

In a once-empty field, the setup team had built a stage made of six-foot-high wooden shipping boxes tied together with heavy rope. Was it rickety? Oh, yes. A five-member band and our team of fifteen seated on white plastic chairs filled the "stage." I was afraid to move, concerned the whole setup would collapse under us.

Large, stacked speakers, piled high, sat on each side of the stage. Their electrical cords, strung from nearby homes, looked like black clotheslines hanging out the windows. A wire was strung between two tall sticks on each side of the stage. One lonely light bulb dangled in the middle, looking as if it were a spotlight for the speaker. The light faded as it reached the sides of the shipping boxes until it was almost totally dark.

With everyone in place, the band struck up the lively music, and the stage began to creak and sway.

Did any of this bother the band? No, not in the slightest. I realized their norm was not mine. They energetically played guitars and drums while passionately singing praises. Wide smiles, dancing eyes, and unswerving faith seemed to indicate this stage would hold without calamity. Their enthusiasm was contagious.

Maybe they know something I don't know, I thought. *Could they be right? Will it last, at least until it is quietly dismantled this evening?* My faith was wobbling with the stage.

Some band members were perched on a sturdier base; others sat on top of the lower-positioned speakers. Every time one of them bounced to the rhythm or swayed with the music, my eyes would dart back and forth, checking the weak joints, bracing myself for a crash, while trying to look calm and unaffected.

Doesn't anyone see the danger? I wondered. *Isn't anyone worried?*

Wouldn't it have been better to put the equipment and the team on the ground somewhere? Couldn't we have accomplished the same goal without all this rickety, tenuous-feeling setup?

And then that lonely light bulb that hung on the wire was positioned so the audience could see who was speaking as the sun set into a dark, starlit night. That made it the main attraction for every bug in the area. As we stood under the light bulb, insects buzzed around our heads, landed in our hair, and found our clothing a perfect resting zone.

Sweating profusely in 93 degree heat and 90 percent humidity, we joined the festive praising. We wiped our faces every couple minutes with handkerchiefs until they were as wet as the heavy air we were breathing. I was praying inside more than I was singing on the outside. *Help me, Jesus, handle this unnerving experience.*

Bugs and More

It was time for Powell to begin his sermon. He jumped to his feet with his interpreter landing forcefully on the weakest, shakiest portion of the stage. Do you think he stood still while telling the people what they needed to know? Of course not. He told the dramatic story of Zacchaeus the tax collector with all the exuberance of the real event, probably with an added pinch.

His interpreter duplicated Powell's every move, doubling the jostling. The interpreter climbed up on one of the fragile plastic chairs, pretending to be Zacchaeus as he tried to see Jesus from his perch in the tree. The audience was entranced with the dramatization. Their wide eyes and gaping mouths validated the power of the story. Obviously, they were eager to hear every tidbit of the fascinating lives of Jesus and Zacchaeus.

Just then a cockroach the size of Maryland (maybe not Maryland, but the size of a rat or a bit smaller) landed next to Powell on the stage. I had never seen such a large cockroach. I barely had enough faith to remain on the shaky stage before the cockroach, but this was ridiculous. *Get me off this stage! I don't want that thing flying or landing near me!* Now I had to add a giant cockroach flying over my head and landing in front of me to my survival skills. I began to fervently pray for more grace so I would not freak out.

Without a break in his story, Powell swung his leg around and kicked the bug, sending it flying. It landed two feet from me, but at least it capsized. I was sure it was staring right at me, though it was upside down with its legs wildly kicking. Knowing nothing about cockroaches, I was convinced it would flip back over onto its feet and fly directly into my lap at any minute. I didn't take my eyes off it for the rest of Powell's message.

No one else on the team had any such experience. We were novice evangelists, which explains why it never occurred to us to move from the exact center of the stage where the greatest density of bugs was congregating. As each person shared their transformation testimony, it seemed logical to stand directly under the lone light. Unlike Pastor Powell, we stood still as we talked about God's life-changing love. Two of us swallowed bugs while speaking. Others were vigorously slapping away bugs from their faces, while trying to share their stories. What an adventure, competing with the insect world for the hearts of these precious Filipinos on Bohol.

Throughout the very buggy, stressful evening, God's precious love for these people was unmistakable. Over four hundred people answered the invitation to receive Jesus as their Savior. Hundreds of healing miracles occurred that night, pain departed, blind eyes were opened, and demonic torment was defeated. But I was convinced we had a miracle as enormous because the stage persevered. It never broke apart.

A New Point of View

As I thought it was time to start packing up all the equipment, the band came back on stage. *What's going on? Aren't we done?* A loud blast from the speakers began the "let's party" music. The drums began banging a dancing beat, the guitars filled the air with lively praise, and the crowd started to bounce. Yes, bounce! Their vertical jumps to each drumbeat were impressive.

Shouting praises, belting out the words, every person in the enormous crowd began to dance. I had never seen anything like it. When they had arrived earlier, they were somber and obviously questioning who we were and why we were there. But now, arm in arm with my team, they twirled, bounced, and danced. The dust from the dry ground filled the air as we celebrated God's incredible transformation until it was time to leave for home.

As the setup and teardown team began their heavy lifting into the trucks, a soft, tropical breeze cooled our sweaty bodies. I was standing near Powell when I heard him ask one of the men to help him get something out of his ear. While he had been preaching, a bug had flown into his ear—and it was still there. I had seen him hit his ear a few times on stage, apparently to get it out. This faithful man hadn't been moved by the annoyance. He stayed on task, doing what he knew needed to be done until it was over, with a bug buzzing around in his ear.

I stared at him incredulously. I had never seen such commitment, such focus. If there was a strong degree of discomfort in other situations I had witnessed, the assumption was God wasn't asking us to continue. This was a different perspective creating a different response.

Difficulty or inconvenience doesn't necessarily mean God is leading us to stop moving. I needed to reevaluate how I thought God revealed his ways. In this setting, in this country, at this time, before these people, finding a more comfortable way wasn't an option. It was a sobering, glorious learning and transforming time, changing my kingdom worldview.

You, Too

The God of all creation is full of surprises for his children.

"I can do all this through him who gives me strength."
(Phil. 4:13)

* * *

How often have you discovered a natural thought was
really a divine directive?

We never know what we will do when we are surprised or even
shocked with the unexpected. Hopefully, you will receive the
needed courage, focus, and God-given perspective that will
enable you to rise to meet the need in any situation.

Lord, thank you that today you haven't asked me to stand on a
rickety stage preaching. But I will, if you ask. I choose to be
willing to do whatever is necessary to fulfill the destiny
you have fashioned for me.

Fishing Village Philippines

Intracultural Evening Philippines

*Laughter workshops
Philippines*

Sri Lanka

India Team Launching
a Movement

India Taj Mahal

Janet Declaring
God's alignment

Victoria Falls, Zambia

India to Sri Lanka to Fiji's Startling Gift

Fiji reconciliation conference

Praying in Siquior for new church plant

Drawing at Malaysian Mall

Marine Coin Vietnam

Women's Cultural Exchange Iraq

Tel Wall at Erbil in Kurdistan

Professors in Duhok University

EXPLOITS FOR GOD

Because He Said . . .

"But the people who know their God shall be strong, and carry out great exploits." (Dan. 11:32, NKJV)

"His intent was that now, through the church, the manifold wisdom of God should be made known to rulers and authorities in the heavenly realms." (Eph. 3:10)

"For our struggle is not against flesh and blood, but against the rulers, against the authorities, against the powers of this dark world and against the spiritual forces of evil in the heavenly realms."
(Eph. 6:12)

* * *

Many women in the Bible have performed great exploits. God empowered slave women, prostitutes, poets, homemakers, beauty contest winners, unmarried mothers, and interracial women as well as members of the royal family, wives of priests, businesswomen, and prophetesses to become bold leaders for him. The stories of a few of them are enough to demonstrate how God chooses and uses women who hear his voice and obey him. Here are some whose exploits are recorded in the Old Testament.

- While the Israelites were enslaved in Egypt, Jochebed was not afraid of the Egyptian king's edict and put her son Moses in a basket in the reeds of the Nile River. When the king's daughter retrieved Moses, Jochebed served as the baby's wet nurse. She birthed one of the greatest leaders in the world.
- By faith born of hearing about the God of Israel, Rahab, a Jericho prostitute, aided Israel's spies and bartered with them for her life and the lives of her family when the attack came. Later, she married Salmon, a Jewish man, and because of her faith was one of the four Gentile women mentioned in Jesus' generational line.
- Deborah, a wife, poet, prophet, and supreme court judge, became an army general and led her people into victory against Israel's enemies.
- Jael, a homemaker, put a peg through the temple of enemy general Sisera as he slept in her tent.
- Esther, a young maiden, was chosen to be among the most beautiful women of the land to become wives of the king. Ignoring a possible death sentence by going to the king without being called, she revealed her identity as a Jew as well as a military leader's plot to destroy her people, saving her entire nation from annihilation.
- Jehosheba, sister to King Ahaziah and wife of a priest, hid her young nephew Joash in the temple for six years to protect him from an illegitimate ruler on the throne of Judah until the boy was old enough to rule, thus preserving the royal seed of David and, ultimately, of the Messiah.

The exploits of New Testament women are equally astounding. Teenaged Mary, Jesus' mother, accepted the shame associated with being pregnant before her wedding to Joseph, by the power of the Holy Spirit, in order to give birth to the Savior of the world. Later, she was a leader in the early church. The stories of the exploits of many other women are recorded also, including those of Anna, Priscilla, Phoebe, Mary Magdalene, and the racially mixed Samaritan woman who introduced Jesus to her people. And women such as Mary and Martha hosted Jesus in their homes, supported, and followed him.

None of these women realized the magnitude of their actions, but they were faithful to do what God put before them. The same is true today, and for the women on our teams. We do whatever we are called to do, in faith, for the One who called us for his purposes.

The Beginning of an Adventure

The year 2000 was a fascinating, interesting, productive, and spiritually successful year for Women With A Mission. We were invited to serve in Germany and Swaziland, where we conducted a Bible study in the queen's palace, and then enjoyed dinner with the king. We were invited to serve in Uganda, Mauritius Island, Singapore, India, Sri Lanka, Hong Kong, Macau, and China during that year also.

In order to accomplish what we were being called to do, we needed to book several trips within a few weeks of each other. I wondered, *How will we be able to manage the costs? The schedule? The number of participants? Simple,* I realized. *Reach out to your core team members, and book tickets going from one country to another.*

Janet and I did that, each buying a round-the-world ticket. We arranged to connect with other team members who would minister in one or more of the counties but were unable to commit to the longer time required for them all.

Janet and I started the year in Germany, and then went to Swaziland as planned. The Swaziland College of Theology had told us it was in dire need of professors. Janet had accepted the invitation to teach on the book of Hebrews, and I was to teach an Old Testament survey course. So that time of ministry was intense as well as productive. Many surprises occurred, including our accommodations in the dated but stately former home of Jimmy Swaggart, who had an exceptional ministry there over many years.

Because other countries were included on the long trip, we couldn't stay the entire semester, so other WWAM team members finished our classes. While our team was together, we conducted a women's conference. It was a wonderful blessing to see so many students from all over Africa, praising God together. All nations and tongues sang together, "You are worthy, our Lord and God, to receive glory and honor and power" (Rev. 4:11).

The star student in my class was Justin from Zambia. His quick smile and laughter were infectious. Known for his ingenious personality, he would try to cause me to reveal what would be on the semester test. Occasionally and for his sake, I would slip in a comment, "Listen carefully. This could be important." I loved the way his eyes would glimmer as his quick hand wrote notes on his tablet.

Justin's phone call several years later surprised me. He said he desired to bless the people of Zambia with a pastor's conference, including special training for women. Within minutes, I agreed to come.

Located in southern Africa, Zambia is a country of rugged terrain and diverse wildlife. It has many parks and safari areas, and the famed Victoria Falls is located at the border of Zambia and Zimbabwe. One side of the waterfall is in Zambia, with Zimbabwe at the bottom, where the Zambezi River continues. It is a marvel, plunging 354 feet into a narrow gorge, with the distinction of being the largest waterfall in the world. The local indigenous name for the Falls is *Mosi-oa-Tunya*, meaning "the smoke that thunders." Renowned missionary David Livingstone, on seeing the massive waterfall, named it after Queen Victoria. I decided I wanted to see Victoria Falls.

A Special Assignment

After our conference in Ndola and before our ministry in Tanzania, we had four free days. Being a maximizer of time during trips, I thought we could do a tour and prayer time at Victoria Falls. I had no idea this time would become the primary purpose of our Zambia visit.

Before the trip, the Spirit began to speak to me about strategy. One Sunday night at church while singing "Praise the Name of Jesus," with the lyrics, "He's my rock / He's my fortress / He's my deliverer / in him shall I trust," I heard the Spirit say, *Stand on a hard rock jutting into the mighty Zambezi River running into the Falls, and make a declaration and proclamation aligning it for the purposes of God.*

I wrote those words down. Why? I knew God would use our team of simple homemakers to do something great.

As I prepared to go, I experienced several more communications from God. I was taking part in a local Bible study group that was studying the science of sound. Once again, while in prayer, I heard the Spirit speak, telling me to buy a tuning fork to use to align Victoria Falls and the Zambezi River to the sound of heaven. This may sound crazy to some people, but I know God's voice. When he speaks, I obey. So I went to the local music store and bought a tuning fork.

While reading my morning devotions shortly before the trip, I read Ecclesiastes 10:20: "Because a bird in the sky may carry your words, and a bird on the wing may report what you say." I was startled. I did not want the enemy to know my strategy for the Falls. Again, I heard a word from the Spirit, with a caution. *Don't tell anyone the plans until you get to the Falls. Otherwise, the enemy could attempt to thwart the plan of God.*

Wow, I thought. *Could I even compose a team without telling them what we would be doing?* I prayed, *God, you can do it.*

While worshiping and taking communion one Sunday morning,

I heard more instruction. It was in the form of a strong impression to worship and give the Zambezi River communion. The instruction from the Spirit was that the team should worship and put small amounts of bread and wine into the river as a prophetic act that the blood of Jesus would be the instrument to bring healing and cleansing to the Zimbabwe people living along the river. I called my good friend Wendi, a pastor in Reno, and asked her to join the team and bring an instrument to play. She accepted gladly. I could share none of these instructions with Wendi.

I had lunch with a woman who has a dynamic deliverance ministry before leaving for the trip. I told her about it without revealing the plans. She looked directly at me and said, "Beware of snakes."

What did that mean? I wondered.

She could not give an explanation, but at that moment she was confident of that warning for me. I wrote it down.

A local woman pastor called me and asked if she could pray over me for our team, to send us out. I drove to her church, where three intercessors waited. After prayer, the pastor said, "I just heard an urgent word for you. When you are finished with what God has instructed you to do, run, *run* out quickly."

Her words reminded me of a story in 2 Kings 9, when Elisha summoned a young prophet to secretly anoint Jehu as the next king of Israel. He told him to take Jehu into a private room away from his friends and anoint him. Elisha continued, "Then open the door and run; don't delay!" (v. 3).

What could this mean for us? I wrote that down, too.

I sensed that God would have a local pastor join us in Zambia. This impression was highly important to me because I believe residents of lands have geographical authority over them. God places his people in the nations of the world for the propagating of the kingdom.

Appointment at the Falls

Several days later, after a long and arduous twenty-one-hour flight and long jeep rides, the team arrived in Ndola. While ministering, we met a powerful, influential woman who was known as the "mama" of Zambia and had active ministry in twenty-five villages. When she inquired of our plans after their conference, I explained our intention to visit Victoria Falls.

Her eyes got big, and she began to shake. "What are you doing there?"

Since the two of us were alone, I explained a part of our plan. Then she told me of the underworld snake god of the Zambezi River, called *Nyami Nyami*, that controlled life in and around it. With a snake for a body and the head of a fish, this snake spirit was believed to protect the local Tonga people. But at times of its anger, floods, death, and destruction followed.

Mama shared that local Christian women would not go near the Falls out of fear. She explained how witch doctors from all over Africa came there to get their power. Even more concerning was the fact that many Christians had confronted this snake god at the Falls and had dropped dead on-site. At that point, I didn't know whether to laugh or cry.

She proceeded to give an interesting perspective on what was happening. She believed that women would be the ones to crush the head of the serpent, and since her country's women feared going to the Falls, God had brought us to do it.

Then she stood, picked up some cloth, and gave me enough for each team member. We were to put the cloth over our heads while doing what God instructed us to do. It would be God's way of hiding us from the snake god. Believe me, I did not mind the idea of hiding from the strongman.

I had arranged for our team to stay in a beautiful resort near the Falls. After we arrived, had lunch, and toured the grounds, I announced that we needed to go to Victoria Falls to do some "spying of the land." The women agreed—and still did not know the plan. I had told them only that we needed to find a large area of land or rock in the river to stand on.

A complete change of mood came over the team, from light-heartedness to a somber realization, as we walked the path together to the site. Along the pathway, we saw several concrete statues of snakes, each overcoming a woman. The one most disturbing was a huge cobra standing up from the bottom of its tail with flared wings. His "arms" displayed a naked woman caught in them. The snake was smiling.

This is the deception of the world, believing that the snake is good and women are to be conquered, I thought.

I knew from studying the Word that the woman was created from the beginning to be a full partner with the man to take dominion over creation (Gen. 1:26). And the Spirit brought to my mind the words of Genesis 3:15 that tell of the seed of the woman, who is Christ, being the One who crushes the snake's head. Seeing that gruesome statue also reminded me of Psalm 91:13, "You will tread on the lion and the cobra; you will trample the great lion and the serpent."

I believe in demonic spirits over nations. Scripture names a handful of them. My friend Fred Markert, the great missiologist with Youth With A Mission, described it in his article in *Charisma Leader*, "Radical Revolution: How prayer, fasting and identification repentance will overcome the power of the Prince of Persia": "They include Leviathan (influences governments), Mammon (influences finances), the Prince of Greece (empowers godless philosophy over societies), and the Prince of Persia (the ruling spirit over Iran, which is 'Persia')."

Our teams do not go intentionally to confront them. We merely do what God has assigned us. In this situation, God had given us multiple instructions. We were to follow our instructions from him.

After arriving at the river, we saw a rock jutting out into the water—black, hard, and large enough to accommodate all eight of us. Having found it and completed our spying of the land, we returned to the resort.

My student friend Justin joined us for dinner. It was good to have this funny man who brings much mirth with us. Also, it was fun to observe his and the team's reactions as I purchased a bottle of red wine. First, I knew drinking wine is not permitted by his church denomination, nor is it allowed on Women With A Mission trips. His surprise in seeing me take it to the room was amusing. He had no idea of the holy purpose for which that wine was intended.

After prayer for cleansing of the room and setting it aside for ministry purposes, I explained the strategy the Lord had given me to the team, beginning with not telling them the plan. We talked about standing on a rock, proclaiming and decreeing to the river, worshiping God, giving the river communion (the bread being miniature pieces of paper with Scriptures), covering our heads, praying in tongues, and sounding the tuning fork. At that moment, team member JoAnne cried out with surprise and grabbed her purse. She reached in and pulled out a tuning fork! God has spoken to her, too, to bring one.

Early the next morning, I instructed our team members to make sure their hotel expenses were paid before we went to the river, and to store their luggage at the front desk as they checked out. I had reserved a bus to pick up us and our luggage at noon. After prayer time and breakfast, we set out for the river, for the rock we had determined to stand on.

Standing on the rock as planned, we began to worship. We placed very small pieces of Scriptures into the river. Then we poured a small amount of the wine into the river, to declare the Lordship of Jesus, and that the nations would serve him. As we reached the end of our praise, it was time for the tuning forks, our last activity.

JoAnne joined me as we made the sound that would be for the alignment, or tuning, of the river. When we finished, we stood for a few seconds until I remembered the Colorado Springs pastor's instruction, "Run, *run* out quickly!"

We started out, walking two by two, to the resort. To our left, running from the south park entrance were fifteen Zambian military men in uniform, carrying guns in front of them. When Wendi saw them, she started strumming her guitar and singing. Somehow, they did not see her.

As we reached the entrance to the park, the attendant said, "Did you see some weird people with head coverings polluting the river? The military is looking for them." Literally within seconds of arriving at the front of the hotel, we loaded our suitcases into the waiting tourist bus and drove off. The last thing I saw was the military brigade entering the resort.

I don't know about the outcome of obeying God at the Falls, but I know how he works—and nothing is without result. Edward Burke once said, "Nobody made a greater mistake than he who did nothing because he could do only a little." Though others may see us as just a few homemakers, God sees us as his obedient and great warriors.

You, Too

In Christ, you are more than a conqueror.

"I planted the seed, Apollos watered it, but God has been making it grow."(1 Cor. 3:6)

* * *

How do you see yourself? How does God see you?

If you are obedient to God, you may rest assured, no matter what he calls you to do, that you are one of his great warriors.

Holy Spirit, you wrote in the book of Daniel that people who know their God will be strong and do exploits. I ask you to bring me into the fullness of knowing you, so that my life will reveal your strength and carry out your glorious exploits.

A STARTLING GIFT

Because He Said . . .

"So, he said to me, 'This is the word of the LORD to Zerubbabel: "Not by might nor by power, but by my Spirit," says the LORD Almighty.'" (Zech. 4:6)

"He heals the brokenhearted and binds up their wounds." (Ps. 147:3)

"Is anyone among you sick? Let them call the elders of the church to pray . . . . And the prayer offered in faith will make the sick person well; the Lord will raise them up. If they have sinned, they will be forgiven." (James 5:14-15)

*   *   *

"Siri, what now?"

Have you ever asked your artificial intelligence device a question and heard the answer, "Beyond my capabilities"? It's a common answer for many of my questions. An AI device has no flexibility or supernatural capability. It only knows what it has been fed.

When I worked for McDonnell Douglas with a high security clearance, quality control mishaps were referred to as GIGO—garbage in, garbage out. I have had to reconsider my personal identity as a believer and leader a multitude of times because the Holy Spirit supersedes the input I received throughout the years.

Healing is one of those experiences that led me to believe I had digested GIGO. Teachings from respected sources decreed that Jesus may have done this in the past, but God no longer heals the physical body or reveals himself in miracles.

My friend Gail, formerly a surgical nurse, said, "I have seen enough to know that we do our best, and it's severely short of what God can do."

That seemed logical to me. After all, he created humankind. He must know how to fix our brokenness. But will he today?

As friends, we decided to practice and see what would happen. Gail's cat was ailing. I can't remember what the obvious problem was, but I do remember her telling the cat a somewhat humorous story. His name was Sam.

"Sam, I'm sorry, but I am not going to take you to the vet. I am practicing to see what God will do, and I am going to start with you. Be healed in Jesus' name." Lo and behold, the cat improved immediately. Only God knows if it was his intervention.

As the Bible instructs, we laid hands on the sick with everyone we knew who had a cough or a severe diagnosis. The recovery percentages began to increase. We discovered healing may be both a process and a miraculous event. Have I seen everyone healed whom I have prayed for since then? No, but I have seen thousands of miracles, enough to know Jesus heals today. Our role is to pray for healings, trusting him with the outcomes (James 5:14; Luke 9:2).

A Prayer for Healing

My first trip to India was with a Women With A Mission team. The team was scheduled to speak in Salem, in south India, at an indigenous mission base. I gazed up at the glorious blue skies overhead as we slowly approached the large auditorium, filled to capacity. When I passed through the door, beauty took my breath away.

Do you know the collective noun for a group of butterflies? It is kaleidoscope. That's what I saw—a kaleidoscope of textures and brilliant colors. Over fifteen hundred women were chatting softly. As I scanned the crowd, my eyes filled with dazzling oranges, vibrant purples, and lemon yellow sari fabrics, cascading over their flowing dark hair and flawless bronze skin. I had never seen such an array of lavish colors. To me, it represented a kaleidoscopic overview of God's women in India.

The stage was approximately thirty feet in depth and stretched more than halfway across the front of the auditorium. Our chairs lined up against the backdrop of a freshly painted picture of Mary washing Jesus' feet. Expectation filled the air as we took our places. We waited our turn to share our heart and message with the women. After break time, it would be my turn.

I had given a copy of my message to my interpreter to read ahead of time, since it was her first time interpreting. During the break, we shared heart to heart and prayed together, asking the Holy Spirit to make us one voice of God's love for the women.

The break time came for afternoon tea. Our team was served a bite to eat and a refreshing drink. As I watched the ladies enjoying their friendly chatter, a woman approached the stage and asked me to pray for her. Her broken English and thick Hindi accent made it difficult to understand what she was asking God to do for her. Her body language and the few words I could understand caused me to guess it was relief from pain. I came to the edge of the stage and reached out for one of her hands. We petitioned our Father God together to meet her need, she in her language and I in mine.

Abruptly, she fell to the cement with a thud. I had seen people succumb under the power of God's presence by falling down, but this time it was so dramatic and sudden, I didn't expect it. At first, I was concerned that something terrible had happened. But as she stood up with a big smile on her face, the woman shared excitedly. I realized Jesus had met her in that moment. Her whole body had submitted to the power of his love. She was healed and was no longer experiencing any pain.

It was a glorious moment for the women standing with us. Like me, they were stunned at first, but then spontaneously we praised our Lord together for this demonstration of his mercy, power, and, yes, his amazing grace.

As you might imagine, other women heard what had happened. They rushed to the stage for prayer. Only a few minutes remained before the break would be over, so I hurriedly prayed with as many as I could. It was one of those "believe, say, repeat" as fast as I could utter the words and reach for them. If only I could have written a prayer for healing and read it again and again as I prayed with each woman individually. It didn't sound like a reverent list of quoted Scriptures or any kind of dramatic presentation. It was simply "Be healed in Jesus' name," again and again. God's presence was so tangible that each lady knew she had been touched and healed.

The call for everyone to take a seat again came too soon. I felt awful that I had to stop praying for those still waiting patiently. When God is saying yes to everything being prayed for in the moment, I don't want to stop. Quickly, I asked one of the interpreters to tell the ladies waiting that after the conference, I would resume praying for the sick. I reluctantly took my seat with the others on stage.

It was my turn to speak. My interpreter Lillian and I took our places behind the pulpit microphone. As I looked down at my notes, one of the Indian leaders whispered in my ear, "Sorry, we must leave very fast after you are done, and we have to cut your time. You only have ten minutes."

When you are being interpreted and are given ten minutes, it means you only have five, because it takes at least equal time, if not a few minutes more, for the interpreter to communicate the concept, translating your words.

I looked down at my notes with a bit of a panicky feeling. I realized I could not communicate effectively the point I had planned to make in that amount of time. What in the world was I going to do? The next thought was what I call a "God thought" or "God idea." At the time I wasn't sure about it, but it was the only idea I had, and I needed an idea in that instant. It was, "You have to leave immediately after this is over, and you won't have time to keep your promise to pray for the women."

I was passionate about keeping my promise. The only thing I had time to do was pray for the women in the audience as a group, asking Father God to meet their needs. I turned to Lillian, and said, "I'm not using my notes. Don't worry. Follow whatever I do, and repeat what I say."

I don't know, and never had a moment afterward to ask Lillian, how the change of plans caused her to feel. I would imagine an inexperienced interpreter who had never spoken before an audience or in a setting like that one would have been startled.

When I work with interpreters, usually I can "feel" them following me. There is a sense of the two of us being one voice and heart. I didn't look at Lillian to see what she was doing as I began to speak, but I could feel her flowing with me. I told the audience the story of God healing a few women at the break. Therefore, I wanted to bless others with his healing, delivering presence. I told them I was going to pray for them then.

After quoting a Scripture that told the story of Jesus healing the sick, I asked everyone in pain to raise a hand. To my shock, hands were raised across the auditorium. Then I prayed what I refer to as "Jesus style." I spoke to the need in the authority of the name of Jesus and pointed to each person around the room: "Be healed in Jesus' name."

After the prayer, I asked, "If you raised your hand, check if the pain is gone. Everyone still in pain, raise your hand again." Only four hands were in the air! To God be the glory for the great things he had done. I prayed again for those four, and the time was up.

The team hustled off the stage to exit the auditorium. I turned around to thank my dear interpreter, who had been so brave and flexible, and to take at least a second to rejoice with her in the goodness of God. I looked around for her and saw her running for her chair. The minute Lillian fell into the chair, her head went down in her lap, and she covered it with her hands. As I ran to her, I realized she was crying. At first, I was deeply concerned. But in a second, the aha flooded my soul. She was overwhelmed at the goodness of God. She said she had never seen miracles like that before. She had never prayed for the sick, expecting miracles, and now she was deep in reverential awe of her Father God and his love for his people.

I knelt in front of her and looked into her eyes. "It was no mistake you were my interpreter. You can do this. God wants you to know it is his will and his power, and you can be an ambassador of his healing."

I repeated those words a couple times, and then I was whisked quickly off the stage.

Meeting Again

The leaders for the next event that day were already coming in. It was an odd feeling knowing that God had been there with us in such a startling, miraculous way, and that this new team of speakers didn't know what had just happened. I had an inner grin as I thought of how we live life, moving along as we know to do, and God comes to us in a surprising moment. He startles, invades, and empowers, showing himself strong, and then we journey on, living our lives as usual once again. It's an intriguing, dynamic, living-in-the-Spirit-of-the-Lord adventure with him.

When I returned home, I shared that wonderful moment with my church and friends. I told them about the interpreter who had been so brave. I declared my sense of God's leading and my faith that he was going to bless her with his ongoing healing presence in her personal ministry. After a month or so, I didn't remember Lillian's name or what she looked like. She was one of many new people I had met, and the trip became a blur of beauty and blessing in my mind.

Four years later, I received an invitation to bring a team to the island of Fiji to speak at women's conferences on relational reconciliation. Fiji has a large Indian population, so I thought it appropriate to have an Indian woman who lived in India on the team. I asked the leader of the ministry in India I had visited to send one. At first, it seemed it would not be possible. Lana made a second appeal on my behalf. Somehow, God opened a way. The leader agreed to send his wife and asked if another woman could accompany her.

I was delighted. It was the obvious work of God that we had two Indian Christian women from India joining our team. The glory of God revealed through those two women is another story for another time—one filled with supernatural opportunities to speak into the lives of a variety of people on that small island through radio broadcasts, conferences, and private gatherings.

One day near the beginning of the trip, I was talking to Pratiba, the woman who had been sent from India, and a memory hit me like an electrical shock. The name of the woman with her was Lillian.

"Pratiba," I asked, "by any wild chance was Lillian my interpreter when I was in India?" I knew the answer before she said it.

"Yes, she was."

I stood stunned for a moment. The woman who had interpreted for me on that glorious day in India was now with me in Fiji. I found her immediately, excited to tell her what a precious memory that time was to me.

"Do you remember, Lillian, that you interpreted for me years ago?"

"Yes, Janet, I do. I want you to know that since that day, God's healing power has been ever-present in my ministry."

You can imagine how I felt in that moment and still do writing this story today. Truly, God is gracious, and his love endures forever.

You, Too

When God leads, he supplies.

"Look at the nations and watch—and be utterly amazed. For I am going to do something in your days that you would not believe, even if you were told." (Hab. 1:5)

* * *

Will you remain flexible and look to the Holy Spirit for direction when circumstances are not what you expected?

Be open, be flexible, and watch God move in and through your life in unexpected ways and circumstances. He may not have you speak to a large audience and experience hundreds of people healed in a moment. But then again, he may. Or his leading for you may be something you would consider small and possibly insignificant. Don't hesitate to follow him. People will experience his goodness through your obedience.

"Now to Him who is able to do exceedingly abundantly above all that we ask or think, according to the power that works in us, to Him be glory in the church by Christ Jesus to all generations, forever and ever. Amen." (Eph. 3:20-21, NJKV)

Island Transformation

Because He Said . . .

"God blessed them and said to them, 'Be fruitful and increase in number: fill the earth and subdue it. Rule over . . .'" (Gen. 1:28)

"Jesus called his twelve disciples to him and gave them authority to drive out impure spirits and to heal every disease and sickness." (Matt. 10:1)

"And these signs will accompany those who believe: In my name they will drive out demons; they will speak in new tongues; they will pick up snakes with their hands; and when they drink deadly poison, it will not hurt them at all; they will place their hands on sick people, and they will get well." (Mark 16:17-18)

*   *   *

We have a mandate—and power. And how brilliant of the Lord to assure us multiple times that we possess spiritual authority because of our belief and trust in him. At the moment of our salvation, he assured us that our new birth meant we were part of his family (Rom. 8:14), possessing his own DNA. Calling us his sons and daughters (2 Cor. 6:18) assured us again of our spiritual authority. And when he gave the great missions mandate, he erased any doubt limiting that authority (Matt. 28:19).

For several years, Tess and Lemuel, pastors and civic leaders on Negros Island, one of our partners in the Philippines, had been asking Janet and me to go to the nearby island of Siquijor, which was infamous for its practice of witchcraft. The church there was suffering greatly, yet years passed before we felt as if we had been given a strategy from God.

In 2001, while I was attending a class on how to reach the lost effectively in my state of Colorado, one of the teachers mentioned in passing that she attributed her group's success in Minnesota to bringing heaven to earth. Their strategy had involved working with both religious and secular leaders. My heart leapt as I began to write a plan in my notebook. Why not invite both secular and ecclesiastical leaders on the island of Siquijor to a banquet?

Recognizing that the island's leaders had spiritual authority over the land, I felt they should be the ones to invite us to visit. I contacted Tess and Lemuel immediately to get their feedback and ask them to contact other pastors to see what they thought about a banquet. To my great surprise and delight, everyone agreed it was not only a good idea, but undertook the work of delivering invitations, which meant crisscrossing dangerous water in a less-than-reliable boat.

Facing the Enemy

After our enthusiastic team landed on the island of Negros several months later, we boarded a rather small fast boat for a 25-mile ride that would allow us to see this beautiful nation of islands. It was dark when we arrived at our destination, Siquijor.

As we exited the rocking boat, we were greeted by a strange sight. An unusual-looking collection of men and women on motorcycles waited on the dock. The men's faces were painted totally black; the women's faces were painted half black. And although cell phones were new at the time, the men had them and were texting expertly. Meanwhile, one motorcycle rider was videotaping. Naively, I thought it was a wonderful greeting from a welcoming family member. Before long, I noticed that the video camera was aimed directly at us.

As we headed out of the seaport gate of the terminal toward a local college where we would be staying, the motorcycle riders followed, darting in and out around our transport. Having been warned by the Holy Spirit that this wasn't merely an annoyance, but instead a spiritual harassment, my first inclination was to ask our hosts to immediately tear down all the banners with our pictures that they had posted around the island. Then I had a sobering thought. Because it was a spiritual battle, tearing down those banners wouldn't make any difference. Instead, we recognized and named what was at work—a Jezebel witchcraft spirit, which manifests as intimidation, manipulation, and domination—and our faith arose. We agreed not to walk in fear.

After arriving at our accommodations, the team settled in for the night. Janet and I had gone out to the beautiful veranda that overlooked the beach to enjoy the glorious, lovely views when the motorcycle gang appeared. This time they were making screeching, honking, and wolf-like howling noises below us. Rather than being unnerved, we experienced an outpouring of holy laughter. It was a spiritual weapon of war (Ps. 126:1-2). The crowd below us became confused. As unlikely as it seemed, God used our laughter to disengage their ridiculous attempts to harass us. The more we laughed, the more the small group began to scatter.

When we returned to our rooms, the other team members were fast asleep, exhausted from the long travel day. I shared a room with Tessie, the national who was our conference leader. After a couple hours, we were awakened abruptly by moaning, crying, and horrific sounds of animals being tortured outside our bedroom window.

At first, I was alarmed, but then the presence and peace of the Lord gave me the strategy for the moment. Was it loud, declarative commands against the enemy? No. We simply put earplugs in and went back to sleep. Miraculously, God gave me an incredible dream showing how to handle this situation the next day.

In my dream, I lifted my skirt above my head, trying to take my dress off in front of my enemy. Then I cried out to the team to pull my dress down, and they did. The enemy started to run away, but I quickly grabbed the leader by the throat and said quietly, "May the Lord bless you. May he rejoice over you and may you be his." Immediately, the leader fell to the ground on his knees. His companions panicked, picked him up, and ran from us in fear.

The dream showed me that God was saying, "Fear not. Treat them with kindness as you would any other guest. Say, 'Good morning, how are you?' as you encounter them. Treat them as you would any other person God loves."

In the morning, I called for a team meeting. The ladies would be more than alarmed when they learned what had happened, and I needed to step up in spiritual authority, with confidence, to address these circumstances. When I mentioned the dream, my daughter-in-law Wella said, "Mom, do you remember when I called you a couple of weeks ago? I had a Scripture for you for the team. We got to talking, getting sidetracked, and I forgot to give it to you."

Then she read aloud Nahum 3:5-7:

> "I am against you," declares the LORD Almighty. "I will lift your skirts over your face. I will show the nations your nakedness and the kingdoms your shame. I will pelt you with filth, I will treat you with contempt and make you a spectacle. All who see you will flee from you."

I was in awe. God had shown me that we were not to walk in fear of this island's spirits, and instead, he would cause them to fear us. In an instant, our team went from fear to faith, and we began rejoicing. We were convinced that God had given us the strategy, the authority, and the victory over the witchcraft.

Another Encounter

As we strolled to our first conference meeting that morning, a gang of warlocks lined the sidewalk leading to the building. We greeted them with sincere smiles, kindness, and warmth, in contrast to the ungodly messages foisted on us. We remained obedient to God's promptings; our ways were his ways, not human ways. The result? The warlocks were completely thrown into confusion. They stepped back, muttered, and walked away.

That evening we held the welcoming banquet. Amazingly, leaders from both secular and religious sectors attended. What a night it was. Anxious pastors, clearly knowing that spiritual beings had been assigned to this island, knew chaos could break out. Governmental leaders wondered what to expect.

I began by thanking them for joining us for this wonderful welcome to their island, resulting in warm exchanges of greetings and handshakes. One government council leader commented from the podium, "Some say that our island is unusual and that we have some unique people on it. But don't worry. If you don't bother them, they won't bother you."

Little did she know that this trip would be one of two kingdoms clashing. I hoped my smile did not betray my thoughts.

The evening went extremely well until we returned to our rooms. Our entire worship team had broken out in hives. Fortunately, both Janet and I had brought Benadryl. We prayed, gave the worship team the medicine, and the next morning, they were well. That was only the beginning of the war between two kingdoms that took place that week. Our visit was an incredible time of God showing himself strong, to give us victory over every evil circumstance manifesting for the remainder of our time.

Only one local pastor had stood on the dock to welcome our

team to the island. When we left Siquijor four days later, more than twenty came, their eyes filled with tears, hugging us as we departed.

I have returned to this island several times since that first visit, and the church is thriving. Many ministries have stepped up to help disciple believers, and pastors are encouraged. And this past year, my team dedicated a new, beautiful church.

Instead of being known as the witchcraft island, Siquijor is now known for quality herbs and natural healing products.

You, Too

Expect the unexpected, and don't limit the Lord.

"'The kingdom of heaven has come near.' Heal the sick, raise the dead, cleanse those who have leprosy, drive out demons. Freely you have received; freely give.'" (Matt. 10:7-8)

* * *

What spiritual battles have you encountered? What direction did the Lord give you? Have you ever considered using laughter as a spiritual weapon?

Don't disqualify yourself because you have not done something before. Instead, use your spiritual authority as a kingdom citizen, seated with him in heavenly places, recognizing its source and limit.

Lord, I know you will equip me for whatever spiritual battles come against me. Help me to be alert and watchful. Remind me that you have already won the battle.

THE POWER OF LIGHT

Because He Said . . .

"One day the evil spirit answered them, 'Jesus I know, and Paul I know about, but who are you?'" (Acts 19:15)

"This is the verdict: Light has come into the world, but people loved darkness instead of light because their deeds were evil." (John 3:19)

*   *   *

Would you be afraid if the devil or his evil spirits said, "I know you"? I trust that wouldn't bring fear, but instead confidence in your authority in the spirit realm, because you have the name of Jesus as your Savior, Lord, brother, and friend.

My friend Kathy and I had been receiving appointments from people who desired prayer for freedom for a couple of years. Two young men whom Jesus had graciously set free from tormenting bondage brought a friend over one evening. The young men were new to Jesus and, outside of their own freedom, didn't have an understanding of the spirit realm, but had easily recognized their friend's need due to their own past.

Jerry looked rattled with fear. "Janet, when we drove up to your house, our friend Gary said in a frightening voice, 'I know these two women.' When he said that, all the hair on my arms and legs stood up with a shock wave riveting down my body at the same time. Should we leave and get him out of here?"

I said encouragingly, "No, it's okay. That's a good thing. That means the devil loses, and Jesus wins."

We declared our authority against the forces of evil that were intimidating Gary, Jerry, and Harold, and welcomed them in. The evening went as we thought it would. We listened to the symptoms of demonization he suffered that resulted in the out-of-control behavior from which he wanted freedom. We explained scriptural foundations for freedom regarding forgiveness and surrendering his life to Jesus as Lord, not only a way out of torment. After his prayer asking Jesus to be his Lord and Savior, we declared Jesus' name over the tormenting spirits, and they left with some dramatic shouts and bodily jerking, in a matter of minutes.

Jesus' name is above every name, and when someone is ready to be forgiven and to forgive, committing their lives to his Lordship, the devil cannot remain. It's a good thing both the enemy to our soul and Jesus know us by name.

Name Above All Names

When I traveled to Manado, the capital city of the Indonesian province of North Sulawesi, it became obvious the dark realm knew me by name. The Dutch missionaries built the first Christian church in Manado called Oude Kerk (Old Church), which still stands and is now called Gereja Sentrum. Manado is a popular spot for scuba diving and snorkeling, especially at Bunaken National Park. Nearby volcanoes and crystal-clear water beckon tourists.

My role was to be one of the intercessors behind the scenes for the island conference. I prayed with the other dedicated men and women of God for many hours, believing our Lord was making a way where there was none for the attendees to be encouraged and empowered from the anointed teaching.

My flight home was a day later than most of the team who were from other countries. A couple of them stayed to scuba dive in the magnificent colorful scenery under the ocean's surface. Since I am not a diver, they asked the wife of a local pastor to take me under her wing for a day and get me to my flight the next. June was bilingual like her young friend Daisy, who picked me up that morning for my tour of the island.

It had been a long but lovely day filled with tropical beauty and delicious dishes to acquaint me with the island's Manadonese meals, typically quite spicy. We traveled up to the top of a high mountain on curvy, narrow roads. On our way down, I was beginning to feel a bit queasy from all the tight turns as we traversed our way back to the hotel, so I lay back to rest for the drive.

We had a professional driver who hadn't said a word the whole day. June, Daisy, and I sat behind him. Leaning back, quieter now, watching the transcendent sunset, we entered the heavy city traffic close to our destination. June began to ask me about the deliverance ministry and how I ministered to people with demonic bondage. We talked about the basic truths of the power of the name of Jesus, the importance of forgiveness, and ensuring the person was ready to make Jesus their Lord, not just removing a level of torment from their lives.

"I understand those principles, but what do you actually say?" she asked.

"When I have ministered truth from the Bible and believe it is time to demand the evil spirits to leave the person, I simply say, 'In the name of Jes—'"

I hadn't even gotten the full name of Jesus out of my mouth when our driver began to scream. His hands flew in the air shaking, and he bounced up and down in his seat, his mind clearly out of control.

It was a dark night filled with heavy traffic and glaring headlights—and our driver was no longer driving the car. Any second, we could have slammed into another vehicle.

In less than a second, I told Daisy, "Take the wheel!"

She flew over the seat, grabbed the steering wheel, and maneuvered the van to the left side of the road. It was a miracle. She had to push herself past his contorting body to get him out of the way so she could pull over safely.

He kept screaming and wildly bouncing until I demanded the devil stop the manifestations. He quieted down immediately. I found out later that the driver was a new believer, and though he had prayed a prayer to be born again, he wasn't yet fully free from the indwelling evil spirits.

June, Daisy, and I spent a brief time talking and praying with him. He didn't speak English, so they interpreted my words as we ministered life to this new brother in the Lord. Notably, the devil could understand me, though our driver could not. He was completely and gloriously set free while we were parked on the side of the road, with blinding bright headlights from the traffic passing by. I left the summation to June since she spoke his language, and soon we drove safely back to drop me off, with goodbyes filled with warm, grateful hugs all around.

June had asked how I ministered to people with demonic bondage. God answered by showing her, "Like this!"

And I couldn't resist telling the devil, "You idiot; I wasn't talking to you."

You, Too

Jesus is the light of the world.

"When Jesus spoke again to the people, he said, 'I am the light of the world. Whoever follows me will never walk in darkness, but will have the light of life.'" (John 8:12)

* * *

Have you turned to Jesus, repenting of any darkness in the past, welcoming the light of this world to overcome the devil's oppression?

If not, fear not. Today is your day. Be forgiven, and forgive. Trust his empowerment and know that no weapon of the evil one will be able to overtake your life.

Lord, I welcome the indwelling Holy Spirit to fill me thoroughly with the light of Jesus, spirit, soul, and body.

Holy Nudges

Because He Said . . .

"Suppose one of you has a hundred sheep and loses one of them. Doesn't he leave the ninety-nine in the open country and go after the lost sheep until he finds it?" (Luke 15:4)

"I tell you that in the same way there will be more rejoicing in heaven over one sinner who repents than over ninety-nine righteous persons who do not need to repent." (Luke 15:7)

*   *   *

The leading of the Holy Spirit emerges in a variety of ways. We have found his nudges don't always appear spiritual at first, but instead feel like an everyday desire. We may want to do this or that, and when we think about it, we don't perceive any reason not to, so we go ahead and act on it.

God can be found in the details of this type of nudging. We have heard people comment that they didn't want to bother God with trivial pursuits. But often a treasure is hiding in what seems like insignificant desires.

The Glorious Ways of God

The Malaysia trip to Koto Kinabalu (KK) is an example of several stories packed within a story. KK, an island of Borneo, is a bustling gateway to the national park, where Malaysia's tallest peak is located. We researched the local botanical garden with the hope we would have time to see its tropical beauty.

The ride from the airport to the hotel didn't provide much of a view except for a few plants with enormous leaves by the roadway. Rest was the highest priority, due to jet lag. As we spent time together the next morning going over the schedule, Helen, the conference convener, had everything ready for us. The room was decorated, the interpreters were assigned, and the worship music was playing softly.

The detail and skill evident in the large, bright lemon-yellow banner mounted on the wall behind the stage was striking and decorative. It featured thousands of hand-sewn sequins, depicting a beautiful Malaysian woman with flowing black hair, nestled in a circle of peaceful white flowers and doves. The intricacy of the detail reminded us of how much attention the Holy Spirit paid each woman who attended.

Janet began her message with our hearts' desire to be the intimate, one-flesh expression of the heartbeat of the living God. She expounded on several questions. What did it mean to be trustworthy like Mary, the mother of Jesus, whose heart was pierced with seven piercings? How do we press into an intimate, loving relationship with our Lord Jesus through truths depicted in the Bible in Solomon's temple by pillars standing before the entrance to the Holy of Holies named Boaz and Jachin, strength and wisdom? The encouragement went beyond receiving a new heart and eternal life into living with his strength and might. In his wisdom we become established and steadfast in the face of our disappointing world, living in his counsel and might. We are the fragrance of Christ.

Lana infused the listeners with hope from James 4, encouraging them that as they drew close to their heavenly Father, he would draw near to them. In 2 Corinthians 11:2, Paul wrote about God's jealous love for us, declaring we are betrothed to one husband, Jesus, and presented as chaste virgins to him. The team's messages encouraged the women to step intentionally into a wholehearted devotion to Christ Jesus.

During the final day, the commitment challenge was to come before the Lord, asking him to purify hearts. The Holy Spirit would enable them to no longer be distracted, double-minded, or over-taken with worry. The call of the Spirit was to be yielded, though their hearts were pierced with sorrow. The Holy Spirit gave them hope that he would be with them at all times. As they made quality choices to love and serve, they would be passing through the symbolic pillars of Boaz and Jachin, strength and wisdom. The Holy Spirit would embolden each one to face troubling times with his presence. Regardless of what would come, he would be with them.

As our messages closed, we asked for the privilege of displaying our love for these precious women by washing their feet. The anointed presence of the Holy Spirit filled not only our hearts, but also the room. We felt honored that we were given the task of talking about the Holy of Holies, that glorious place where the fullness of the Spirit of God dwelt in Solomon's temple, accompanied by his presence filling our room that day. We were energized, and at the same time, we had a deep desire to lie prostrate on the floor, motionless.

The Holy Spirit impacted these women in such measure, the local conference leaders said everyone needed a rest to absorb all that the Holy Spirit had imparted during our times together. As the afternoon passed, we slowly returned to our rooms.

Drawing a Picture of Christ

After resting a bit, I (Janet) had a desire to see more Malaysians and something beyond the walls of the conference room.

"Lana, this place is famous for shopping and beauty, and we have no time to see or do anything. I want to rush over to the mall next door and at least see something different for the forty-five minutes we have available. Would you go with me?"

"Sure, let's go." Lana is always ready to go to a shopping mall.

We had just entered the shopping area when I noticed a man sitting by an easel selling his sketching talent. I immediately thought, *Have your picture drawn.*

I didn't want to take the time, nor did I want a picture of myself. But the thought kept coming, nagging me, until I decided reluctantly that it might be the Holy Spirit.

"Lana, I think I am supposed to have that guy draw me. I don't know why, but I have to see what the Holy Spirit is up to."

I sat down, introduced myself, and asked the price. "I don't have much time, so this will have to be fast. And please do not draw me years younger than I am. I have seen other sketches of women who always want to look at least ten years younger than they are. I want it to look like I do today."

He stopped, staring at me for a moment with a curious look on his face. "I have never had anyone say that to me. May I ask, why are you so comfortable with your age?"

That was the open door to tell him what it means to have your core identity in Christ Jesus. As he was sketching, I talked to him about being transformed by the loving ways of a living God. He asked the questions we all would love to be asked: "How can I be saved?" "How can I know this living and loving God?" "What do I need to do?"

As we were sharing heart to heart, Lana noticed the mall police watching us. Visible guns slung around their front presented an intimidating sight. Lana moved closer and whispered, "You are being watched."

We lowered our voices a bit, but his curiosity was so engaging, I couldn't stop sharing Jesus. Lana came even closer to act as a shield so no one could see clearly or hear our conversation easily. As the sketch artist prayed, giving his life to Jesus, confessing his sins, and welcoming the Holy Spirit, the security police were coming to question us. Before they arrived, however, my sketch was completed.

We shared grateful smiles and handshakes, and we scampered off to the next meeting.

We were happy, happy, happy as we bounced our way through the doors to our seats once again. Helen sat by us, and I joyfully told her of our adventure. Also, I gave her information on how to find the man in the mall.

She replied, "It may be a plant. It may not be a true salvation. Often they try to trick us by asking all the right questions because it's illegal here to openly proselytize. If it is not genuine, they will arrest us. But don't worry; they will only deport you."

As you may imagine, that encouragement didn't help my sinking emotions. I couldn't wait to hear what they would discover. I was prayerfully trusting the sketch artist would still be there so they could question him.

To my great relief, they returned with good news. It was a valid salvation. They made the connection and had plans to get together in the near future.

The Holy Spirit knew there was one among all those people roaming the mall, one who was ready to hear and receive. It was a nagging nudge to have my picture drawn. It seemed frivolous, a waste of money and time. But I decided to follow the nudge in case it was the Spirit. He knows what will motivate us to want what he wants, and do what he desires. Ultimately, we get the incredible gift of watching him accomplish what only he can do—save lives.

You, Too

God is a loving Father.

"The Lord is not slow in keeping his promise, as some understand slowness. Instead he is patient with you, not wanting anyone to perish, but everyone to come to repentance." (2 Pet. 3:9)

* * *

Are you ready to step into a life-giving journey with him as you listen to the beat of his heart?

The joy of the Lord is your strength. In your choices you will find joy, though it may happen among piercing tears. Disappointments come in this life. But in and through it all, God's wisdom and strength will uphold and lead the way.

Holy Spirit, I am asking you to heal me of all my personal wounds and bring clarity and understanding to any and all blind spots in my thinking.

Privilege, Purpose, Priorities, and Pleasure

Because He Said . . .

"Jesus replied, 'What is impossible with man is possible with God.'" (Luke 18:27)

"You will show me the path of life; in Your presence is fullness of joy; in Your right hand there are pleasures forevermore."
(Ps. 16:11, AMP)

*   *   *

Answering the question "Who am I?" may be a continual treasure hunt. Evaluating our abilities and inabilities can be both encouraging and discouraging at the same time. What are we to expect in life from our personal identity and influence? I have found that without the input from God's Word and the guidance of the Holy Spirit, it falls drastically short of my true potential. I remain dependent upon the Holy Spirit's intervention, while at the same time I trust not only our relationship, but his caring for people far exceeding my own. What has been a confusing, threatening, or frustrating journey in my efforts to hear his voice has folded into a deep, abiding thankfulness. His providence turns my meager efforts into something beautiful and blessed as only he could do.

Often I shake my head in amazement, feeling stunned at the

deep impact the work of evangelism and short-term missions has had in my life and that of my family. It's been years since my first taste of serving God in another culture and location. I was shaking, with no idea if I could be effective. Yet I couldn't wait to step out and see what God would do. Trained? No. Qualified in any way? Not in my estimation. But the setting and expectations I was invited into didn't call for more than love for God and a heart to help people. I was willing and excited to give it a try. I wasn't sure of my life purpose in this area of ministry. But the momentary purpose was to help others discover what I had found true, the love of God through his Son Jesus Christ.

Every year has had new adventures in grace that cause me to be deeply grateful for God's willingness to fulfill his sacrificial love as I reach out to people.

New Delights

Finding the purpose of one trip at a time expanded into a life purpose and fervent passion. It has not only changed my personal priorities regarding what I do, where I go, and who I am with, but it also transformed the way my husband and I spend our money and more. As privileges unfolded, priorities changed, and as priorities changed, so did my purposes for life and how I receive pleasure.

It remains treasured fun for Tom and me to play games with our grandchildren, spend a relaxing day enjoying beautiful scenery together, or visit with our adult children. And shopping is always enjoyable for us gals, whether children or grandchildren.

I continue the privilege of traveling with Lana and ministering with Dona, Fran, Pat, JoAnne, Marnie, and many others. Intercessors like Shannon, our intercession coordinator, keep us covered in prayer through our unique and diverse travels. Pivotal national and international leaders have encouraged my process of understanding God's calling in my life, such as pastors and evangelists Romey and

Nora Corpuz, pastors Jill and Luz Boyonas, Powell Lemons, Naomi Dowdy, Rick Wright, Marnie Piuze, and my husband, Tom.

Some of my deepest "doing" (active) pleasures come from God's ministry opportunities. I have had the privilege of standing before a large outdoor audience feeling a nearly indescribable, overshadowing love from Father God for each person. I have watched him straighten broken parts, take away pain, and defeat the demonic realm harassing people, resulting in lives transformed by the inworking and eternally saving Holy Spirit.

The love God has placed graciously in my heart for humankind expanded into personal friendships in other countries as well as at home. What I take pleasure in now aligns with my life purpose, which, in turn, makes the priorities a pleasure, not a responsibility or duty.

God Loves All of Us

One of my treasured memories is speaking at a small gathering of thirty to thirty-five people in Japan. Again, I was astounded at the privilege of being a representative of Jesus. These people worked in a nightclub and had stayed up all night for our arrival and presentation. Their lifestyles were varied, with a majority in a transvestite life from male to female, available for a price. As our pianist played the bar piano in powerful, atmosphere-changing worship, they sat wide-eyed, intently listening. I couldn't tell if some of them were male or female, but what I knew was that God loved them, Jesus died for them, and he was willing to bring the eternal, powerful work of transformation into their lives. My privilege and purpose in those few minutes was to be a bridge to that opportunity.

When my turn came to share, I began by describing how people were attracted to Jesus by his unconditional love. I shared Bible stories of those compelled to follow and listen to his words as he walked the dusty roads of his day.

As I described the sacrifices he made to be with people, I could see the audience leaning forward, receiving the words, obviously stunned, yet open. I offered his invitation into eternal life. One by one, they slowly moved toward me to pray, and then a few at a time quietly followed. They waited patiently for their turn to ask God for his eternal life and shared prayer requests for a variety of needs.

After I led them in a heartfelt salvation prayer, one person asked, "Can God undo what I have done?" How would you have answered? My heart was deeply moved by the question. I wanted to wrap my arms around all of them in a long, tight hug.

Everything within me was crying out for God to reveal his unconditional love to these precious ones. I responded the best I could in the moment. I felt God's incredible, abiding love for each one. "He begins in our hearts where eternity dwells," I said.

They continued to come forward for prayer until all but one in the room had said yes to Jesus. We invited them to church, where I would be speaking. Smiles, chatting, warm hugs, and goodbyes followed before we packed up and went to a home where we would get rest.

The next day was Sunday, and guess where they were? As they entered the church where I would be speaking that morning, they were convinced of our friendship, acceptance, and God's love. Where would you sit if you had never been in church before? You would look for your friends and sit next to them. They sat down in the front row next to me. I was barely able to contain my joy. It was a new beginning with a new Spirit filling their spirit. Their learning experience had begun like mine had so many years before regarding their eternal purpose and destiny, fulfilled alone by their heavenly Father.

I am and ever will be deeply touched that God has allowed me such a privilege, purpose, priority, and pleasure as he did that day. Every time I experience such a gift from him, whether thousands or few are in the audience, I remember the simple questions I asked

God and the simple answers he gave in return years ago when it first began.

The transformations of these people have become my personal transformation. To God be the glory. May it never end until I see Jesus face to face.

You, Too

God empowers his children to become ambassadors of his love.

"My dear children, for whom I am again in the pains of child-birth until Christ is formed in you." (Gal. 4:19)

* * *

Are you willing to share the Good News of the kingdom of God with those unlike yourself?

Time with God will prepare you to speak truth in love to those you never dreamed would be listening. Fear not. Think (focus on) caring love before exacting correction. The Holy Spirit is more than able to bring someone out of their unhealthy thinking and lifestyle into a healthy way to enjoy life. We have the Holy Spirit's wisdom to share God's heart as well as his directives, leading people into the kingdom of God as only he can do.

Lord, lead me into your will and plan for my life through obedience, prayer, and listening to the Holy Spirit. Help me gain understanding for my life.

THE AROMA OF CHRIST

Because He Said . . .

"When Solomon finished praying, fire came down from heaven and consumed the burnt offering and the sacrifices, and the glory of the LORD filled the temple. The priests could not enter the temple of the LORD because the glory of the LORD filled it." (2 Chron. 7:1-2)

"She had to complete twelve months of beauty treatments . . . six months with oil of myrrh and six with perfumes and cosmetics. And this is how she would go to the king." (Esther 2:12-13)

"Then Mary took about a pint of pure nard, an expensive perfume; she poured it on Jesus' feet and wiped his feet with her hair. And the house was filled with the fragrance of the perfume." (John 12:3)

*   *   *

The Bible has many references to fragrances and sweet-smelling oils, including incense, nard, and myrrh. The most well-known are those connected with worship, love, and burial. Incense was used in the tabernacle for worship as a sweet-smelling invitation to the Spirit of the Lord. Perfumes were used to prepare Esther to be with the king. The book of Song of Songs includes many references to the smells in the palace bedrooms and gardens. Myrrh was one of the gifts the wise men from the East brought to the Christ Child. Possibly the most famous reference is Mary anointing Jesus with nard before his death and burial.

It is noteworthy that in 2 Corinthians 2:15-16, the apostle Paul used aroma as an analogy for the effect Christ's followers have on others: "For we are to God the pleasing aroma of Christ among those who are being saved and those who perishing. To the one we are an aroma that brings death; to the other, an aroma that brings life."

The implication was clear to the Corinthians. Whenever Rome conquered a new land, its defeated leader was taken to Rome to be paraded before the people. The conquering general rode a white horse, and the captured leader was placed directly behind him and paraded naked through the streets. At the same time, a sweet perfume would be released to represent the "sweet smell of victory." However, to the enemies of Rome, it was the smell of defeat and death.

In 1995, my dear pastor friend Nora in the Philippines invited me to join her in a ministry trip to Malaysia. Her sister resided there, and she desired to conduct a women's conference. It would take place in the city of Koto Kinabalu, located on Borneo Island, the third-largest island in the world and the largest in Asia. I accepted without hesitation. I had no idea what to expect. What an adventure was in store for us.

Change Me

Upon our arrival, we were whisked away to a stately hotel close to the beach. Our elegant rooms had breathtaking views of the ocean. The conference room reserved for our meetings was beyond regal. The meetings were to be confined to the hotel, and we were to have no public display of activities. Islam was and is the official religion, and legally, all Malays are Muslim.

During one morning meeting, Janet preached on Mary, sister of Lazarus and Martha, and how she showed her extreme devotion to Jesus while he was visiting and teaching in their home. She explained that at one point, Mary sat at Jesus' feet and broke a soft, translucent alabaster box filled with expensive nard oil. She poured it over his feet, an extravagant and unusual act, because typically, oil was poured on the head, and she used her hair to wipe his feet. Also, it was shocking because in those days a respectable woman would not unbind her hair in public.

As Janet was speaking to the approximately three hundred women, I noticed an amazing odor filling the room, unlike anything I had smelled before. It was similar to the scent of gardenia, a most fragrant, pleasing smell. I was sitting in the front row on the left-hand side of the room next to the middle aisle. Our team, with Pastor Nora on the last seat, was on my left. I looked across at her, and she was smiling, pointing to her nose. I lifted both open hands in front of me slightly, pointed to Janet, and smiled.

I knew that Janet loved to preach illustrative sermons. When the aroma began, at first I assumed that she had made arrangements with the hotel staff to put perfume in the air-conditioning system. I watched and listened for what she would say next, but she continued preaching with no acknowledgment of the scent.

Shortly after the aroma began, one by one the ladies in the room began to slip off their chairs. Some kneeled, and some lay before the Lord. Within minutes, every woman was on the floor, crying gently. It was as though a potent gas had entered the room. But instead, I realized it was the presence of the Lord overpowering them. There were no loud noises or movement. It was a time of quiet awe.

The glory of the Lord had completely filled that place. He was ministering to the women, meeting all their needs. They were experiencing the aroma of his powerful presence. As with the priests in 2 Chronicles 7:2, nothing else could happen. His presence encompassed that place totally. Janet and our team walked around the room, praying over the women. Most were basking in the Holy Spirit.

After the service, the conference leadership asked if we could cancel the afternoon meeting. They said the women wanted to go to their rooms and continue to process their experience that morning. Of course, we agreed. We all came together one last time that evening, and the conference was over.

As the women were basking there, I was reminded of the words of the song "Change Me" by Shannon Wexelberg:

> Here in the light of Your presence
> I see how Holy You are
> I'm bowing down, Lord, in reverence
> You know my heart
> You have become my Desire
> Teach me to walk in Your ways
> Come now and cleanse me with fire
> This prayer I pray [1]

---

[1] Words and music by Shannon Wexelberg Adducci. Copyright 2007 Shanny Banny Music/BMI. ShannonAdducciMusic.com. Used by permission.

You, Too

The presence of the Lord supersedes anything else we can experience in this life.

"Better is one day in your courts than a thousand elsewhere; I would rather be a doorkeeper in the house of my God than dwell in the tents of the wicked." (Ps. 84:10)

"Do not forget to show hospitality to strangers, for by so doing some have shown hospitality to angels without knowing it." (Heb. 13:2)

* * *

Have you ever experienced unusual manifestations of the presence of the Lord? If not, are you open to experience new intimacy with his love?

God rarely used the same method twice in the Bible. Look for fresh expressions of his grace and mercy to be unveiled. Be open to angelic activity as Scripture has indicated.

Yes, Lord, I am excited to embrace the new and creative ways you reveal yourself in this hour.

THE COIN, FORGIVENESS, AND SERVANTHOOD

Because He Said . . .

"For the Holy Spirit will teach you in that very hour what you ought to say." (Luke 12:12, NKJV)

"But those who hope in the LORD will renew their strength. They will soar on wings like eagles; they will run and not grow weary; they will walk and not be faint." (Isa. 40:31)

"The greatest among you will be your servant." (Matt. 23:11)

*   *   *

Lana was forming a team to teach Bible scholars and leaders in Vietnam. I had qualifying credentials, but I wasn't sure of the type of messages that should be developed for such an educated audience. I wasn't sure if I should go, but I said yes.

As I was preparing to be a team member, I asked one of my dear friends, Pastor Bill Peters, to pray for my time in Vietnam. He is a decorated US marine who led special ops teams into Vietnam years ago. I knew he would have a heart to pray for me, but I had no idea of the drama I would experience because of my friendship with him.

An Ambassador of Forgiveness

Bill served in Vietnam in 1969 with the First Force Reconnaissance Company, an elite special operations group. His time in-country was action-packed, running twenty-three long-range patrols deep into enemy-controlled territory in the central highlands of Vietnam. His missions were designed to gather firsthand intelligence on the movement of the enemy. His injuries in enemy-controlled territory brought him close to death.

This experience left a deep impression on him that the Holy Spirit turned into a man seeking life beyond death. It led him into Holy Spirit–driven Jesus encounters, transforming him into gratefully serving Jesus Christ in full-time ministry for over fifty years.

Bill, his wife, Barbara, and I sat on their couch as I explained I was headed to an underground Christian outreach in Vietnam. Suddenly, he stood up and quickly left the room without saying a word. I looked at Barbara, puzzled. She just smiled.

He returned with something in his hand. "Janet, this is a special honor coin bearing the Marine Corps globe and anchor emblem. I believe you will be able to discretely bury the coin in the land as a peace offering for the blood on both sides of that ten-year war. When you do, say a prayer on my behalf, asking for forgiveness and healing regarding myself personally and our nation's role in the fight. I have been asked to return to Vietnam as a minister on several occasions. I can't make myself say yes. This act might make it possible for me to return and minister to the wonderful Vietnamese people. Be my ambassador of love and forgiveness in Jesus' name and authority, please."

The three of us prayed that the Holy Spirit would lead me to a prophetic act of forgiveness and to become an ambassador of peace as I joined the team.

A Challenging Mission

Many restrictions were in place on our discussions during travel and around the hotel. It was serious and yet amusing when we would converse normally, and suddenly one of the team would remind us to talk quietly with shushing.

Apparently, these leaders had never had women preachers speak in a seminar setting. We were a paradigm shift in everything we said or did that day. I don't believe the Vietnamese leaders were aware that our team's preachers and teachers were female. John, the head of the ministerial association, began making the introductions and within minutes several men got up and walked out. A handful of others turned their backs on us as we began to speak. Often, I wondered how the women in the audience felt during this obvious rejection of a female teaching males.

Each day in Vietnam was filled with sights, including the war museum, which was covered in hatred for Americans, as well as the reawakening beauty of the flora and fauna. I kept an eye out for the right place to bury the significant coin and pray over the land, as Bill had requested. By the time the seminar was to begin, I still hadn't found a good place to discretely bury it, and pray for peace and forgiveness.

I was scheduled to be the last speaker at the seminar. Sandy, our main team intercessor, was asked to give her testimony. Gloriously, God had delivered her recently from over $1 million in debt. Her freedom from financial bondage had been progressive. In a moment of creative inspiration, she asked for several of the colorful plastic chairs to be brought to the front. She began her story of widowhood, poverty, and despair as she sat behind the microphone on a plastic chair. Sandy is a slightly built woman of approximately one hundred pounds. She shared how God began her freedom and the difficult faith choices along the way.

As she told the story of each new event that separated her from the deep debt, she put one of the plastic chairs on top of the others, and climbed up to be seated. Her very slight frame was now resting a little bit higher as she continued her story. With each decision of faith, each glorious deliverance story, she rose from sitting on a single chair to several chairs high. As she rose one chair higher, she repeated, "Focus on hope. Faith will grow."

It was a brilliant visual. No one else on the team could have climbed up and rested on that many precarious plastic chairs. The audience was without expression the entire time she was speaking. Were they interested? Upset? Bored?

She quoted her last Scripture, gave her appeal to rest in faith, and sat down. When she did, the men jumped to their feet, heading straight for the stage. They couldn't wait to sit on those chairs. They wanted to express their faith by resting on a chair, to declare their ongoing reliance on God's upcoming provisions. The women in the audience began to weep. We sat stunned at the final responses. They had been listening intently and absorbing her testimony, challenged and encouraged to go higher in faith.

Time was running out, and it was Pastor Wendi's turn. It was becoming clear there would be no time for me to share my message.

Wendi was teaching on living a life of servanthood in the kingdom of God. She had a creative idea: "Let's do a pantomime. I will not only teach a principle, but act out a scene between two women. You will become offended, reject me, and make it clear to the audience you are very upset. With gestures only, try to convince the audience not to listen to me while I am teaching. At the end, I will wash your feet as a gesture of serving. We obviously forgive one another, smiling, hugging, and visually restored in relationship."

It was a terrific, spontaneous idea that took us ten minutes to develop. Again, we had the audience's rapt attention.

When it was time to close the seminar, John, the ministerial leader, came over to say thank you. "We have never had anyone illustrate a message by acting it out. We loved it. The visual presentation helped the message have practical applications." And then he offered a quiet apology. "Please forgive us for not showing our pleasure and interest on our faces. We have been trained over the years to show no emotion. We are overcome with joy at the presentations today."

Suddenly, I remembered the coin. "I have a coin from a marine who served in Vietnam in special ops. He asked me to bury it and ask forgiveness on his behalf," I explained. "I can't find a place to bury it. Could you suggest a place? He is a follower of Jesus and a pastor in California."

John lit up. "Don't bury it. Give it to me. I will take it with me each time I am speaking with the pastors and leaders. I will tell Bill's story, and how he is asking our forgiveness for the bloodshed. It will be a powerful tool God will use to bring forgiveness, mercy, and healing."

I asked John if he would let me record his forgiveness to share with Bill when I returned home. He happily looked into the camera. "Bill, we forgive you and your teams. Brother Bill, we invite you to return to Vietnam as a brother in Christ."

I pondered my role for the days in Vietnam, and the time and finances required to join the team. I asked God to forgive me if I didn't make the right choice. But if it was his leading, it would be a gift to have him confirm it to me. I sat on the plane traveling home, pondering the way my interaction had unfolded in Vietnam. *Did you send me, Lord, merely to be part of a skit on living a serving life and giving a coin to a leader?*

God's Purpose

When I returned home, I couldn't wait to have time with Bill and Barbara Peters. We sat in their living room, sharing the beauty of the people, the sadness of their hearts, and the hope for the future in the youth of the land. I was thrilled to show them the video on my phone. I was so eager for him to see it, I felt like a child waiting to open a surprise birthday gift.

As Bill watched Rev. John, tears flowed from his eyes. He described a burden lifting from his soul and a lightness in his being from the Holy Spirit's interaction that day. He softly said, "Now, I can return if God leads."

A warm, sweet feeling came over my soul. I believe it was Father God's message to my heart, encouraging me that these two opportunities alone were enough to make the trip of great value in the heavenly realm. That made it worth it all.

You, Too

If you focus on hope, faith will grow.

"But as for me, I watch in hope for the LORD, I wait for God my Savior; my God will hear me." (Mic. 7:7)

"Love must be sincere. Hate what is evil; cling to what is good. Be devoted to one another in love. Honor one another above yourselves . . . . Be joyful in hope, patient in affliction, faithful in prayer. Share with the Lord's people who are in need. Practice hospitality." (Rom. 12:9-10, 12-13)

* * *

You may have days when you say yes to serving but aren't sure of the value of the time, money, and effort you have spent. We won't always know exactly what the Holy Spirit is up to, or how he values an act of serving. We do know willingness will grant blessings as we continue to serve his love for people.

Lord, help me to remain open to serving, even when I can't see the outcome.

THE ANTIDOTE FOR
SELF-DISQUALIFICATION

Because He Said . . .

"Open wide your mouth and I will fill it." (Ps. 81:10)

*"Now when they bring you to the synagogues and magistrates
and authorities, do not worry about how or what you should
answer, or what you should say. For the Holy Spirit will
teach you in that very hour what you ought to say."*
(Luke 12:11-12, NKJV)

*   *   *

The entire twelfth chapter of the Gospel of Luke addresses the attitudes and mindset followers of Jesus are to have. Jesus told his disciples to be on guard, to be dressed and ready for service, and not to be afraid or worry. Jesus advised the disciples how to respond when facing persecution and other difficult situations. He offered them his antidote for possible feelings of doubt and inadequacy. He warned them that they would face leaders in the civic arena, in the temples, and other authorities. But he promised the Holy Spirit would enable them to have adequate answers when they were called to speak.

Perhaps the disciples were concerned that their own skillfulness in words and defense might injure, rather than complement, the truth of the gospel. Maybe they were feeling self-disqualification.

Jesus the teacher knew they would experience fear, stress, anxiety, and other crippling emotions. He prepared them for their future.

On the Spot

I found myself facing these emotions when I was in Kurdistan in northern Iraq. It was 2011, and our team had been sent to the University of Duhok for a women's cultural exchange. I was standing in front of a lectern, feeling panic and despair about my ability to face the arena to which God had called me.

Fear had me totally in its grip. I had believed we would engage female students in an informal cultural meeting regarding women's issues. Not so! Looking over my audience, I saw the university president and other male professors sitting in the front rows, while only a few women sat in the back of the room. I was surrounded by men with postgraduate degrees from Oxford and Cambridge.

Usually, I do not sweat, but that day my blouse was wet with perspiration. I felt as if I had to dance on the head of a pin. My heart was pounding, and I could hardly breathe. Nothing in my formal education had prepared me for such an occasion. My knowledge of Middle Eastern values and customs was practically nil. I was very concerned that I would offend my audience, not to mention the fear that my language skills, words, and expressions would be interpreted as not very intelligent.

My mind was racing. *What can I present?* My teachings were mostly sermons. But as I stood praying under my breath, I remembered a small book I had read years before, *Foreign to Familiar: A Guide to Understanding Hot- and Cold-Climate Cultures* by Sarah A. Lanier. Miraculously, I remembered that I had a PowerPoint presentation for the book on my computer. I praised God silently for his provision.

The book is based on a theory that the population of the entire world may be divided into two arenas: hot-climate or relationship-based cultures and cold-climate or task-oriented cultures. Since Middle Eastern countries are hot cultures, and America is a cold culture, I decided to discuss some of the differences, and how they affect women and children.

I stepped out in boldness, opened my computer, and the list of all my sermons popped up. I moved quickly out of that file—or that is what I thought. But the same file popped up three times. Can you imagine my chagrin? Eventually, I decided I would not use the presentation. I closed my computer and chose to speak without it. My silent prayer was, *Lord, help me remember the five main points.*

An Opportunity for the Gospel

As I started to speak, my eyes fell on pastor and team member Wendi, who was seated at a table near my left. She opened her computer and turned it my way. She had an outline of that entire book in front of me. What a sigh of relief! I spent the next forty-five minutes lecturing with some degree of coherency.

At one point, a man asked, "Are you telling us that we are inherently different due to the weather?"

I smiled, cocked my head, lifted up my hands, and said, "Yes."

Everyone laughed, and I felt a great relief. I explained that I was under the impression that I would be meeting with women only that day. I asked if the men could be dismissed, so our team of women could meet with only the women students present. One man in the back of the room stood up and said, "Why not?"

When the man began walking out, thankfully every other man followed him. As he passed by me, he smiled broadly and winked. I was sure he knew I was a missionary and was aiding me in my predicament. I can say that I have experienced what Jesus taught in Luke 12. In my inadequacy, the Holy Spirit showed up and revealed what I ought to say.

The cultural exchange time with the Iraqi women went very well. I was praying that circumstances would allow for some discussions of the gospel, and that is exactly what happened.

Later, our team was able to interact with approximately thirty women. One issue raised was the lack of freedom that women experienced in each country. One woman, who recently had graduated with her doctorate degree, questioned why women enjoyed greater liberties in the West, providing us with the opportunity to explain the United States Constitution was based on Judeo-Christian values. Since we were behind closed doors, the women admitted that the restraints placed on them were due primarily to their religious system.

As our team was leaving the university, a journalist and television reporter came running up to us with camera in hand. He was shouting in *Sorani,* the Iraqi language, and waving his hands. He had a woman interpreter with him, who explained that he wanted an interview for the evening news.

"Why are you here in our country to try to bring your Western infidel ideas to our women?" he shouted loudly. "Who invited you here?"

"We were invited by your Ministry of Higher Education," I replied.

Then he yelled, "You are nothing but troublemakers!"

In that instant, I remembered an encounter between Ahab and Elijah, recorded in 1 Kings 18. Ahab said to Elijah, "Is that you, you troubler of Israel?" and Elijah answered, "I have not made trouble for Israel, but you and your father's house have" (vv. 17-18).

I replied with confidence, "We have not troubled Kurdistan. However, you have brought trouble by shouting at invited guests."

Then his phone rang, he answered it and left quickly along with his interpreter. Our team's presence was on the evening news, but it was a positive report about American women coming to initiate a relationship with Iraqi women.

God Directed Our Steps

How this trip to the biblically significant nation of Iraq came to be is a story unto itself, as are the exploits that God put before us during the rest of our time there.

Our team's invitation came from Sharon, one of my family members, residing in Erbil, the capital of Kurdistan. She was working as an advisor to the Kurdistan Regional Government. Not only a beautiful, strong, and creative woman, Sharon has been a Fulbright Scholar thrice, in Russia (Moscow State University), China (People's University of China, Beijing), and Japan (University of the Ryukyus). She has a Master's in Religious Studies, Doctor of Jurisprudence, Doctor of Philosophy (Sociology), and Master of Law and Letters. Her position in Erbil was Academic International Liaison and Advisor on Human Rights. Her association with the Ministry of Higher Education and Scientific Research led to our invitation.

We arrived at the Erbil International Airport with great anticipation and were greeted with high fives and laughter. The airport was new, but small. The airport "employees" were soldiers from the United States, some shouting, "Welcome to Iraq!"

The Kurds in Erbil are the largest people group in the world without a country. They have an extremely turbulent history, but are also strong, powerful warriors, willing to fight for their survival. Because the U.S. military was present in Iraq as a peacekeeping force, the Kurds were hospitable toward Americans. Oddly, the airport did not have a customs area to go through or security checks for our team, so it took little time to get to the baggage area.

Our visit began with a welcome from the vice president of Kurdistan. He was a kind, gentle man who offered us the customary Middle Eastern hospitality tea. The hot water was poured from a beautiful silver samovar, found throughout Russia and the Middle East. Our small, highly decorated glasses were presented to us as a gift.

Traveling to our college dorm accommodations, we noticed the landscape, flat desert and one color—sand, arid with little evidence of rain. It was hot and sunny outside, typical for that part of the world. Behind colorfully painted large gates, however, were beautiful green yards and flower gardens.

One day during our visit, the temperature reached one of the highest recorded temperatures in Iraq during a horrific sandstorm. The sand blew into our rooms through the panes of the windows. As I looked outside, I could not see anything but a thick, brown wall. Even inside our rooms, we had difficulty breathing. I remember discovering sand in my bed that evening.

Erbil is a modern, beautiful city, teeming with diverse people. The residents are filled with life and very welcoming. Giant pubs and restaurants are everywhere, as well as many tandoori shops. When we went to the large square in the center of the city, vendors readily gave away their products. And we had multiple opportunities for picture taking. Shoppers were approximately 80 percent male. Women were rarely seen outside the large indoor bazaar.

Above the square, on the north side of the city, is a large hill, an ancient *tel*, or mound, comprised of eight civilizations that built one upon another. The wall surrounding the citadel is impressive as well, being approximately 105 feet tall and believed to be six thousand years old, making Erbil one of the oldest continuously inhabited cities in the world.

We decided to visit the tel. As we approached the entrance gate to the citadel, I became violently ill. Of course, I was embarrassed. After I regained my strength, we continued our tour. We came upon an archeological dig in progress to uncover a temple thought to be one of oldest in the world. It was believed to be the temple to the goddess Semiramis, said to be the wife of Nimrod, a descendant of Ham and Noah.

Trustworthy sources have called this mystical woman, or spirit, Ishtar, Astarte, Ashtaroth, Artemis, and Isis. She is also called the

Queen of Heaven. Israel was warned repeatedly in the Old Testament to reject the worshiping of these evil spirits. Our guide mentioned that when I became ill suddenly, she believed God was using me as a prophetic sign that God himself was vomiting out the practice of goddess worship.

Our ministry schedule was intense. We taught in a newly established underground Bible school, preached at a large Assyrian Christian church, went on tours escorted by the president's mother, and toured amazing sights on our own. At one point, we were asked if we would visit Halabjah, where approximately fifteen thousand people were gassed by Saddam Hussein and buried in a huge mass grave. We were asked to pray over the families for God's recompense. It was said that Hussein destroyed 4,500 villages, 150 of them Assyrian Christian villages.

My favorite visit was to a compound in process of restoration and not yet open to the public, believed to be the site of the prophet Nahum's burial. A wire fence surrounded the workplace. We approached the workmen at the guard shack, showed them our passports, and said, "We have come from America to see this place. Would you please let us in?" It was noontime, and the workers were taking a break, so we were allowed a few minutes to see the work progress. We visited the chapel inside and sang some worship songs over the mountains and wide plains of Nineveh below.

Nahum was the prophet in the Old Testament who prophesied to the people of Nineveh. From Nahum's monastery, built on a high mountain, we could see the site of the ancient city, today known as Mosul. Wide, flat open plains stretched on each side of it. With active imaginations, we looked upon the huge plain where a major exodus of Jews took place. It was 1951 when the migration called Operation Ezra and Nehemiah occurred. The number seems unsure, but some references say over fifty thousand Jews left Iraq. Today, few Jews remain in the entire country.

On the trip home, we were able to spend time touring Petra in

Jordan. What a blessing and truly a wonder of the world it is to behold. Once again, God gave us an unexpected opportunity.

None of us may know the eternal significance of our experience on that trip to Iraq. The same can be said for our other missions trips. However, we are sure that we place our feet on the ground and believe God will use it as a prophetic act. When we are called to go, we go boldly, empowered by what Jesus said in Luke 12.

You, Too

The Holy Spirit will teach you what you need to know and do in the hour you need it.

"They triumphed over him by the blood of the Lamb and by the word of their testimony." (Rev. 12:11)

* * *

Do you trust the Holy Spirit to show up when you are overwhelmed?

You must be open to the leading of the Holy Spirit and speak up when you have the opportunity. Remember, it is by the word of your testimony that you will overcome Satan.

Lord, when I am weak, you are strong. When I am hopeless, you bring hope. Help me in the times I feel overwhelmed, and bring life out of confusion.

Ordinary Women Bringing Freedom

Because He Said . . .

"I have given you authority to trample on snakes and scorpions and to overcome all the power of the enemy; nothing will harm you." (Luke 10:19)

"The weapons we fight with are not the weapons of the world. On the contrary, they have divine power to demolish strongholds. We demolish arguments and every pretension that sets itself up against the knowledge of God."
(2 Cor. 10:4-5)

*   *   *

Spiritual warfare is not what I seek when my teams go out to minister. But it happens, and we deal with it as God directs. When we are called upon, we have to stand against Satan in the authority of Christ. Our three main weapons are his name, the blood of Christ, and the Word. Because encounters with evil spirits happen so often on my trips, I studied the Bible and found at least forty-two spiritual weapons are applied in Scripture—including singing.

Breaking Bondage with Song

The pastor was confused. The congregation was embarrassed. The team was praying, and I was on the floor struggling physically to shut down the manifestations of an evil spirit.

It happened at the end of our team's three-day conference at a large international church in Japan. The pastors had scheduled a time of worship and prayer for Sunday evening. Everyone had gone to the front of the sanctuary and was on their knees praying. The beautiful blonde pianist, also the church co-pastor, had finished her piano worship. She put on a worship music CD and went to a pew to kneel and pray. As she knelt, a young woman from the congregation went to her. I watched as a troublesome conversation ensued. The pastor hurried over to me and asked if I would minister to the young woman.

I crawled over to "Janelle" and asked if I could pray with her. She looked at me with a skewed face and answered with a man's voice, "You will not!"

Then she raised her left arm and tried to hit me with her closed fist. I was able to block it, but she grabbed my arm. Before I could react, she threw me to the floor. She fell on her back and started writhing and pushing her feet, like a snake trying to get away from me. Since she was a small woman, I managed to restrain her, with the Holy Spirit's help. Janelle's eyes remained closed throughout the entire encounter.

In a deep, throaty voice, the demon argued with me, declaring I had no authority over it. Though Janelle was totally out of it, she kept sticking her tongue in and out of her mouth, looking like Gene Simmons of the rock band KISS.

"Don't stick out your tongue at me," I said. "I am a daughter of the most high God."

At that point, my team member Sandy saw what was happening and joined us on the floor. Interestingly, Janelle was not able to get her tongue out of her mouth again, but the demon still spoke. "I will not come out, and you can't make me."

"The sacrifice of Jesus will bring you out!" I declared.

Then the demon cried out loudly, "Don't say Jesus!"

I mocked him by saying, "Jesus, Jesus, Jesus." Janelle began to convulse violently, and I realized that my words had caused pain. Through her, the demon spat at me.

What now? I thought.

The demon addressed me again. "I have had her for seventeen years."

"That's nothing," I responded. "The Lord has had her since the foundation of the world."

"She will worship me," he responded.

Janelle and I were in the middle aisle of the church. The head pastor was on his knees at a nearby pew, watching our every move. I recalled that it was Janelle who had led worship that morning and understood the connection. The demon himself wanted her worship. I responded boldly, "She will worship the true and living God! His blood has bought her. It will free her."

"Don't talk about the blood!" he yelled loudly in a guttural voice.

I realized what I needed to do, but I needed a partner. *Where is my team member JoAnne?* I thought. *She is gifted with such a beautiful singing voice.*

I looked up and saw JoAnne walking around the perimeter of the church, praying. I caught her eye and motioned for her to join me. When she came over, I asked her to sing with me "Oh, The Blood of Jesus."

In the story of Jehoshaphat, recorded in 2 Chronicles 20, a mighty army came against Israel. At the king's command, the people sang, and the Lord set ambushes against the enemy. Singing worship was the key to their victory. It destroyed and annihilated the invading army.

When JoAnne and I began singing, the demon begged to be

left alone. Janelle's body reacted as well. The movement began in her groin and worked its way upward toward her face. Her stomach bloated, her chest got large, and her neck soon looked like a swollen kickball. I realized she was about to expel the demon.

Sandy, who had remained on the floor with us, bolted up and ran to a large cardboard sign on a bulletin board, ripped it off, and placed it under Janelle's head. As we watched, Janelle's eyes became swollen and bulging, like a huge frog. Then the screeching started. Finally, she vomited. It was over.

Janelle lay on the floor a few seconds longer, softly crying. Then she opened her eyes. "Why am I on the floor?" she asked weakly. She had no concept of what had just happened to her. Then her husband came and assisted her to the ladies' room.

The Aftermath

The head pastor of the church, who had witnessed it all, asked me to explain to the congregation what had just happened. I referred to Luke 13:10-17, the story of the woman in the synagogue who was bent over with a spirit of infirmity for eighteen years. Jesus healed her with these words, "Woman, you are set free from your infirmity." (v. 12). Jesus called her a daughter of Abraham. She was in covenant relationship with God, yet she was crippled by a spirit of infirmity.

This was only one example of Jesus healing those experiencing spiritual bondage, I explained. As humans, we are body, soul, and spirit. As the body may have physical ailments, the soul may have bondages. I explained that Christians can "give place" to the devil in their lives. Paul mentioned it in Ephesians 4:27: "Do not give the devil a foothold." This kind of oppression may cause strange or extreme behavior, personality changes, defeat, a sense of failure, depression, self-inflicted injury, and suicide.

After the service, I gave Janelle and her husband a handout on how to stay clean that included several directives. The three most important ones were to read the Word daily, pray to the Father, and fellowship with other saints. Being committed to purity was on the list as well, which includes guarding what we watch, what we hear, and what we think upon. We must focus our thinking on what is true and noble, whatever is lovely, and on good reports. If anything is praiseworthy, we should think on those things. Above all, we must be quick to repent (my paraphrase of Philippians 4:8).

As our team debriefed with the pastors the next morning, the lead pastor, affiliated with a denomination that had doctrinal beliefs that did not include what had happened the night before, said, "I would have never believed this unless I saw it with my own eyes."

Later I learned that Janelle had been traumatized at the age of seventeen. The evil strongman entered through a series of traumatic rejections. The spirit of rejection overtook her soul over the years. From time to time, before that day, she had acted strangely, most recently at the church picnic. No one had recognized what was happening. Personally, I believe that our team threatened the demon, and he manifested that evening. I thank the incredible, loving God that he set this woman free.

Aren't we called to do the same?

You, Too

God is a merciful deliverer.

"He has sent me to proclaim freedom for the prisoners and recovery of sight for the blind, to set the oppressed free." (Luke 4:18)

* * *

Are there people in your life you need to forgive to keep your freedom in him?

Forgiveness is key to freedom. It's not about an emotional feeling, but a choice of your will to obey the Word of God. In time, your feelings will line up, and these things will cause you to grow and become stronger in the faith.

Lord, forgive me for my inability to recognize that I am carrying grudges from past hurts and disappointments. Set me free from any permissions I have inadvertently given the enemy over my mind. Holy Spirit, fill those spaces with your unconditional acceptance.

Rev. Dr. Lana Heightley is an ordained minister with a masters and a doctorate diploma. She is the president and founder of Women With A Mission (WWAM), has been working in world missions for thirty-five years, sharing the gospel and discipling believers. Her passion is team ministry, raising up teams of "ordinary" women to use their spiritual gifts in teaching, discipling, training, equipping, and empowering men and women around the world to become spiritual leaders in their nations. Here and abroad, she is a mentor to countless pastors and emerging leaders.

Lana is the author of two books, *Presents From On High: Freeing Women to Walk in Their Gifts,* and *Divine Assignments: You Have One Too!*

Rev. Dr. Melonie *Janet* Mangum is an ordained minister with two doctorate degrees in theology. Since 1993, she has worked with outreach teams of all ages and ethnicities, both developing the team members as well as leading teams that train and equip in numerous nations. She has served as an associate pastor and interim senior pastor. She is the founder and president of Partners for Transformation, Director of Transformation serving in Aglow International, and is the author of *Until I See: Light On The Path While Caring for Those with Special Needs*; *Selah: First Glimpse*, and *Selah: The View from Both Sides*.

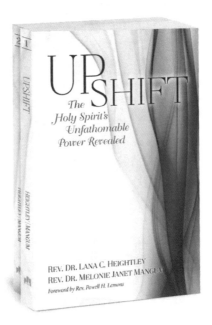